THE AUSTRALIAN
Women's Weekly

If I had to single out a particular subject for which the food pages in *The Australian Women's Weekly* are best known, it would have to be desserts. It's obvious from your calls and letters that you're suckers for sweets... just like myself and all the Test Kitchen home economists! So, believe me, it was with great pleasure that we spent an inordinate amount of time salivating over past issues' dessert pages to come up with this delectable selection. I hope you enjoy making these treats as much as we did choosing them for you.

Pamela Clark

Food Director

contents

BLACKBERRY AND APPLE PIE

PREPARATION TIME 50 MINUTES (PLUS REFRIGERATION TIME) **COOKING TIME** 1 HOUR 5 MINUTES

We used golden delicious apples in this recipe.

9 medium apples (1.4kg)
2 tablespoons caster sugar
1 tablespoon cornflour
1 tablespoon water
300g frozen blackberries
1 tablespoon cornflour, extra
1 tablespoon demerara sugar

PASTRY

2 cups (300g) plain flour
²/₃ cup (110g) icing sugar
   mixture
185g cold butter, chopped
2 egg yolks
1 tablespoon iced water,
   approximately

1 Peel and core apples; slice thinly. Place in large saucepan with caster sugar; cook, covered, over low heat, about 10 minutes or until apples are just tender. Strain over small saucepan; reserve cooking liquid. Blend cornflour with the water, stir into reserved cooking liquid over heat until mixture boils and thickens. Place apples in large bowl, gently stir in cornflour mixture.

2 Meanwhile, make pastry.

3 Toss blackberries in extra cornflour; stir gently into apple mixture.

4 Spoon fruit mixture into pastry case; top with rolled pastry. Press edges together, trim with knife; decorate edge. Brush pastry with a little water; sprinkle with demerara sugar. Using knife, make three cuts in top of pastry to allow steam to escape. Place pie on oven tray; bake, uncovered, in hot oven 20 minutes. Reduce oven temperature to moderately hot; bake, uncovered, in moderately hot oven about 30 minutes or until pastry is browned lightly. Stand 10 minutes before serving.

PASTRY Blend or process flour, icing sugar and butter until combined. Add egg yolks and enough of the water to make ingredients just come together. Knead dough on floured surface until smooth. Refrigerate 30 minutes. Roll two-thirds of the dough between sheets of baking paper until large enough to line greased 23cm pie dish. Ease dough into dish; trim edge. Cover; refrigerate 30 minutes. Preheat oven to hot. Roll remaining pastry between sheets of baking paper until large enough to cover pie.

serves 8
tip This recipe is best made on the day of serving. For a different flavour, replace blackberries with blueberries, raspberries or strawberries.

BUTTERMILK PANCAKES WITH WHIPPED PRALINE BUTTER

PREPARATION TIME 15 MINUTES **COOKING TIME** 15 MINUTES
Vienna almonds are toffee-coated almonds available from selected
supermarkets, nut stands, and gourmet food and specialty confectionery stores.

2 cups (300g) self-raising flour
1/3 cup (75g) caster sugar
2 eggs, separated
30g butter, melted
1 teaspoon vanilla extract
2 cups (500ml) buttermilk
3/4 cup (180ml) maple syrup

WHIPPED PRALINE BUTTER
125g butter, softened
1 tablespoon icing sugar mixture
1 tablespoon maple syrup
1/3 cup (45g) vienna almonds, chopped coarsely

1 Make whipped praline butter.
2 Combine flour and sugar in large bowl; whisk in combined egg yolks, butter,
   extract and buttermilk.
3 Beat egg whites in small bowl with electric mixer until soft peaks form. Fold
   a third of the egg white into batter, then fold in remaining egg white.
4 Pour 1/4 cup of the batter into large heated non-stick frying pan; cook, over
   medium heat, until browned lightly both sides. Repeat with remaining batter.
   Serve pancakes with maple syrup and whipped praline butter.
   WHIPPED PRALINE BUTTER Beat butter in small bowl with electric mixer
   until pale in colour. Beat in sugar and syrup; fold in nuts.

serves 4

PANETTONE BREAD AND BUTTER PUDDING

PREPARATION TIME 20 MINUTES (PLUS STANDING TIME) **COOKING TIME** 1 HOUR 45 MINUTES

Panettone is a sweet Italian yeast bread and can be found at most gourmet delicatessens.
Fruit bread can be used instead.

1kg panettone
90g butter, softened
1 litre (4 cups) milk
300ml thickened cream
$^2/_3$ cup (150g) caster sugar
1 vanilla bean
3 egg yolks
3 eggs
¼ cup (80g) apricot jam
1 tablespoon orange-flavoured liqueur

1 Preheat oven to moderately slow. Grease deep 22cm-round cake pan; line base and side with baking paper.

2 Cut panettone in half from top to bottom (reserve half for another use); cut remaining half in half again, then crossways into 1.5cm slices. Toast panettone lightly both sides; spread one side of each slice with butter while still warm. Slightly overlap panettone slices around edge of prepared pan; layer remaining slices over base of pan.

3 Combine milk, cream and sugar in medium saucepan. Split vanilla bean in half lengthways; scrape seeds into saucepan, then place pod in saucepan. Stir over heat until mixture boils. Strain into large heatproof jug; discard pod. Cover; cool 10 minutes.

4 Beat egg yolks and eggs in medium bowl with electric mixer until thick and creamy. Gradually beat in hot milk mixture; pour custard over panettone in pan.

5 Place pan in large baking dish; add enough boiling water to dish to come halfway up side of pan. Bake, uncovered, in moderately slow oven about 1 hour 30 minutes or until custard sets; stand in pan 30 minutes. Carefully turn pudding onto wire rack; turn top-side up onto serving plate.

6 Stir jam and liqueur in small saucepan over heat until combined; strain. Brush jam mixture over warm pudding.

serves 8

tips This recipe is best if made on the day of serving, but will keep for up to 2 days.
You can use Cointreau, Grand Marnier, Curaçao or any other orange-flavoured liqueur in this recipe.
Replace the liqueur with water for a non-alcoholic dessert.

POACHED PEARS IN RED WINE SYRUP WITH PEAR CRISPS

PREPARATION TIME 20 MINUTES (PLUS REFRIGERATION TIME)
COOKING TIME 2 HOURS 15 MINUTES

6 medium pears (1.4kg)
2 cups (500ml) water
2 cups (500ml) dry red wine
½ cup (125ml) orange-flavoured liqueur
4 strips orange rind
¾ cup (165g) caster sugar
1 vanilla bean

PEAR CRISPS
1 medium pear (230g)
½ cup (110g) caster sugar
½ cup (125ml) water

1 Make pear crisps.
2 Meanwhile, peel pears, leaving stems intact.
3 Combine the water, wine, liqueur, rind and sugar in large saucepan. Split vanilla bean in half lengthways; scrape seeds into pan, place pod in pan. Stir over heat, without boiling, until sugar dissolves. Add pears; bring to a boil. Reduce heat; simmer, covered, about 1 hour or until pears are just tender.
4 Transfer pears to large bowl; bring syrup to a boil. Reduce heat; simmer, uncovered, about 10 minutes or until syrup reduces by a third. Remove from heat; discard pod.
5 Strain syrup over pears, cover; refrigerate 2 hours or until cold.
6 Divide pears and pear crisps among serving plates; drizzle with syrup.

PEAR CRISPS Preheat oven to very slow. Line oven tray with baking paper. Using mandoline, V-slicer or sharp knife, cut unpeeled pear into 2mm slices. Stir sugar and the water in medium saucepan over heat, without boiling, until sugar dissolves; bring to a boil. Boil, uncovered, about 5 minutes or until syrup thickens slightly. Add pear slices, reduce heat; simmer, uncovered, about 5 minutes or until pear is just tender, drain. Arrange pear slices, in single layer, on prepared tray. Bake in very slow oven about 2 hours or until dried, turning occasionally. Cool about 15 minutes or until crisp.

serves 6
tips We used packham pears for this recipe; they should fit snugly, standing upright, in the saucepan.
If pear syrup is too sweet, you can add about a teaspoon of lemon juice.
You can use Cointreau, Grand Marnier, Curaçao or any other orange-flavoured liqueur in this recipe.
serving suggestion Serve with nut-flavoured ice-cream.

ORANGE AND RASPBERRY SELF-SAUCING PUDDING

PREPARATION TIME 5 MINUTES **COOKING TIME** 15 MINUTES

This quick and easy version of the classic recipe does not require pots or pans, so it's the perfect dessert for pudding lovers with no time to waste.

¼ cup (20g) flaked almonds
30g butter
¾ cup (110g) self-raising flour
⅓ cup (80ml) milk
⅔ cup (150g) firmly packed brown sugar
2 teaspoons finely grated orange rind
¾ cup (110g) frozen raspberries
¼ cup (60ml) orange juice
¾ cup (180ml) boiling water

1 Grease shallow 1.5-litre (6-cup) microwave-safe dish.
2 Place nuts in small microwave-safe bowl; cook, uncovered, in microwave oven on HIGH (100%) about 2 minutes or until browned lightly.
3 Place butter in medium microwave-safe bowl; cook, uncovered, in microwave oven on HIGH (100%) 30 seconds. Add flour, milk and half of the sugar; whisk until smooth. Stir in rind and raspberries; spread into prepared dish.
4 Sprinkle remaining sugar over raspberry mixture; carefully pour over combined juice and boiling water.
5 Place pudding on microwave-safe rack; cook, uncovered, in microwave oven on MEDIUM-HIGH (70%-80%) about 12 minutes. Stand 5 minutes.
6 Sprinkle pudding with nuts. Serve with cream or ice-cream, if desired.

serves 4
tips If cooking in a conventional oven, grease 1.5-litre (6-cup) ovenproof dish. Bake, uncovered, in moderately hot oven about 20 minutes.
This recipe is best made close to serving.

COFFEE AND PECAN PUDDINGS WITH CARAMEL SAUCE

PREPARATION TIME 15 MINUTES **COOKING TIME** 40 MINUTES

¾ cup (90g) coarsely chopped toasted pecans
300ml cream
1½ cups (330g) firmly packed brown sugar
100g cold butter, chopped
125g butter, softened
1 teaspoon vanilla extract
½ cup (110g) caster sugar
2 eggs
1 cup (150g) self-raising flour
¼ cup (35g) plain flour
¼ cup (60ml) milk
1 tablespoon finely ground espresso coffee

1 Preheat oven to moderate. Grease six ¾-cup (180ml) metal moulds or ovenproof dishes; line bases with baking paper.
2 Divide nuts among moulds; place moulds on oven tray.
3 Stir cream, brown sugar and chopped butter in small saucepan over heat, without boiling, until sugar dissolves. Reduce heat; simmer, uncovered, without stirring, about 5 minutes or until mixture thickens slightly. Spoon 2 tablespoons of the sauce over nuts in each mould; reserve remaining sauce.
4 Beat softened butter, extract and caster sugar in small bowl with electric mixer until light and fluffy. Add eggs, one at a time, beating until just combined between additions. Stir in sifted flours, milk and coffee; divide mixture among moulds. Bake, uncovered, in moderate oven 30 minutes. Stand puddings 5 minutes before turning onto serving plates.
5 Reheat reserved sauce. Serve puddings with sauce.

serves 6
tip The caramel sauce and puddings can be made several hours ahead and reheated before serving.
serving suggestion Serve with cream or ice-cream, if desired.

TIRAMISU CAKE

PREPARATION TIME 45 MINUTES (PLUS REFRIGERATION TIME) **COOKING TIME** 25 MINUTES

Originally from Sicily, marsala is a sweet fortified wine; you can substitute it with any coffee-flavoured liqueur if you prefer. Mascarpone, an Italian fresh soft cheese, can be found in the dairy section of your supermarket.

6 eggs
1½ cups (330g) caster sugar
1 cup (150g) self-raising flour
½ cup (75g) cornflour
1 cup (250ml) boiling water
1½ tablespoons instant coffee powder
¾ cup (180ml) marsala
4 egg yolks
2 cups (500g) mascarpone
¼ cup (25g) finely grated dark eating
  chocolate
300ml thickened cream
75g dark eating chocolate, extra

1 Preheat oven to moderate. Grease two deep 19cm-square cake pans; line bases with baking paper.

2 Beat eggs in medium bowl with electric mixer about 10 minutes or until thick and creamy. Add 1 cup of the sugar, 1 tablespoon at a time, beating until sugar dissolves between additions. Gently fold in triple-sifted flours, then ¼ cup of the boiling water. Divide mixture evenly between prepared pans; bake, uncovered, in moderate oven about 25 minutes. Turn cakes immediately onto wire racks to cool.

3 Meanwhile, combine remaining boiling water, coffee and ½ cup of the marsala in small bowl; cool.

4 Beat egg yolks and remaining sugar in small bowl with electric mixer until thick and creamy. Add remaining marsala and mascarpone; beat until combined.

5 Line deep 19cm-square cake pan with plastic wrap. Split cooled cakes in half horizontally; place one layer of cake in pan, brush with ⅓ cup of the coffee mixture. Spread with 1 cup of the mascarpone mixture; sprinkle with 1 tablespoon of the grated chocolate. Repeat layering, finishing with layer of cake, cover; refrigerate 3 hours or overnight.

6 Beat cream in small bowl with electric mixer until soft peaks form. Turn cake onto serving plate; spread top and sides with cream. Using vegetable peeler, make chocolate curls from extra chocolate; sprinkle over cake.

serves 12

tip This recipe can be made 2 days in advance and kept, covered, in the refrigerator.

LIME MERINGUE PIE

PREPARATION TIME 15 MINUTES (PLUS REFRIGERATION TIME)
COOKING TIME 15 MINUTES

250g plain sweet biscuits
100g unsalted butter, melted
½ cup (75g) wheaten cornflour
1½ cups (330g) caster sugar
½ cup (125ml) lime juice
1¼ cups (310ml) water
60g unsalted butter, extra
4 eggs, separated
2 teaspoons finely grated lime rind

1   Grease 24cm-round loose-based flan tin.
2   Blend or process biscuits until mixture resembles fine breadcrumbs. Add butter; process until combined.
3   Using one hand, press biscuit mixture evenly over base and 2cm up the side of prepared tin, place on oven tray; refrigerate while preparing filling.
4   Combine cornflour and ½ cup of the sugar in medium saucepan; gradually stir in juice and the water until smooth. Cook, stirring, over high heat until mixture boils and thickens. Reduce heat; simmer, stirring, 1 minute. Remove from heat; stir in extra butter, then yolks and rind. Continue stirring until butter melts. Cool 10 minutes.
5   Spread filling over biscuit base, cover; refrigerate 2 hours.
6   Preheat oven to moderately hot.
7   Beat egg whites in small bowl with electric mixer until soft peaks form; gradually add remaining sugar, 1 tablespoon at a time, beating until sugar dissolves between additions.
8   Roughen surface of filling with a fork before spreading with meringue mixture. Bake, uncovered, in moderately hot oven about 5 minutes or until meringue is browned lightly.

serves 10
tip   The base and lime filling can be made and assembled up to 1 day in advance.

HONEY-ALMOND PASTRIES

PREPARATION TIME 45 MINUTES **COOKING TIME** 15 MINUTES

1½ cups (240g) toasted blanched almonds
½ cup (110g) caster sugar
1 teaspoon ground cinnamon
30g butter, softened
1 tablespoon orange flower water
8 sheets fillo pastry
100g butter, melted
1 cup (360g) honey
1 tablespoon toasted sesame seeds

1 Preheat oven to moderate. Grease two oven trays.
2 Blend or process almonds, sugar, cinnamon, softened butter and
  3 teaspoons of the orange flower water until mixture forms a paste.
3 Cut fillo sheets in half lengthways, then in half crossways; cover fillo
  rectangles with baking paper, then with damp tea towel. Brush one fillo
  rectangle with melted butter; using hands, roll 1 level tablespoon of the
  almond mixture into log shape. Place log at short end of fillo rectangle;
  roll to enclose mixture, folding in sides after first complete turn. Brush
  with melted butter. Repeat with remaining fillo rectangles, melted butter
  and almond mixture.
4 Place pastries, seam-side down, on prepared trays. Bake, uncovered, in
  moderate oven about 15 minutes.
5 Meanwhile, bring honey and remaining orange flower water to a boil in
  medium saucepan. Reduce heat; simmer, uncovered, 3 minutes.
6 Add hot pastries, in batches, to honey mixture, turning until well coated; drain
  on greased wire rack. Sprinkle with seeds; cool completely before serving.

makes 32

CINNAMON FLAN

PREPARATION TIME 15 MINUTES (PLUS STANDING AND REFRIGERATION TIMES)
COOKING TIME 1 HOUR

This recipe must be made 24 hours in advance to allow toffee to dissolve.

1 cup (220g) caster sugar
½ cup (125ml) water
2½ cups (625ml) milk
300ml thickened cream
2 cinnamon sticks
2 cloves
4 eggs
2 egg yolks
⅓ cup (75g) caster sugar, extra
2 teaspoons vanilla extract

1 Preheat oven to moderately slow.
2 Stir sugar and the water in medium heavy-based saucepan over heat, without boiling, until sugar dissolves; bring to a boil. Reduce heat; simmer, uncovered, without stirring, until syrup is golden brown in colour. Pour syrup over base of deep 20cm-round cake pan. Place pan in large baking dish (toffee will set at this stage).
3 Combine milk, cream and spices in medium saucepan; bring to a boil. Remove from heat, cover; stand 15 minutes. Strain milk mixture; discard spices.
4 Whisk eggs, egg yolks, extra sugar and extract in medium bowl. Gradually whisk warm milk mixture into egg mixture, strain mixture over toffee in pan. Pour enough boiling water into baking dish to come halfway up side of pan. Bake, uncovered, in moderately slow oven about 45 minutes or until custard just sets. Remove pan from water; cool. Cover; refrigerate 24 hours.
5 Just before serving, turn flan onto a rimmed serving dish.

serves 8

TARTE TATIN

PREPARATION TIME 40 MINUTES (PLUS REFRIGERATION TIME) **COOKING TIME** 1 HOUR 45 MINUTES

Tarte tatin is traditionally made in a heavy cast-iron frying pan with an ovenproof handle. The pan is covered with pastry once the apples have caramelised, and then transferred directly to the oven for baking. We have adapted the recipe to allow it to be cooked without such a pan. Pears or quinces can be used instead of apples, if desired.

6 large apples (1.2kg)
100g unsalted butter, chopped
1 cup (220g) firmly packed brown sugar
2 tablespoons lemon juice

PASTRY

1 cup (150g) plain flour
2 tablespoons caster sugar
80g cold unsalted butter, chopped
2 tablespoons sour cream

1 Peel, core and quarter apples. Melt butter in large heavy-based frying pan; add apple, sprinkle evenly with sugar and juice. Cook, uncovered, over low heat, 1 hour, turning apple as it caramelises.

2 Place apple, rounded-sides down, in 23cm pie dish; drizzle with 1 tablespoon of the caramel in pan. Reserve remaining caramel. Pack apple tightly to avoid any gaps, cover; refrigerate while preparing pastry.

3 Make pastry.

4 Preheat oven to moderately hot.

5 Roll dough between sheets of baking paper until large enough to cover apple. Peel away one sheet of baking paper; invert pastry over apple. Remove remaining paper; tuck pastry around apple. Bake, uncovered, in moderately hot oven about 30 minutes or until browned. Carefully turn onto serving plate.

6 Reheat reserved caramel over low heat; drizzle over apple.
   PASTRY Process flour, sugar, butter and sour cream until ingredients just come together. Knead dough on floured surface until smooth. Cover; refrigerate 30 minutes.

serves 8
tip You may need to use a simmer mat or cover the pan occasionally while the apple is caramelising to prevent the evaporation of too much liquid and subsequent burning.
serving suggestion Serve warm tart with cream or ice-cream, if desired.

UPSIDE-DOWN TOFFEE BANANA CAKE

PREPARATION TIME 15 MINUTES **COOKING TIME** 55 MINUTES

You need two large overripe bananas weighing about 460g to make 1 cup of mashed banana.

1 cup (220g) caster sugar
1 cup (250ml) water
2 medium bananas (400g), sliced thinly
2 eggs, beaten lightly
²/₃ cup (160ml) vegetable oil
¾ cup (165g) firmly packed brown sugar
1 teaspoon vanilla extract
²/₃ cup (100g) plain flour
¹/₃ cup (50g) wholemeal self-raising flour
2 teaspoons mixed spice
1 teaspoon bicarbonate of soda
1 cup mashed banana

1 Preheat oven to moderate. Grease deep 22cm-round cake pan; line base with baking paper.

2 Stir caster sugar and the water in medium saucepan over heat, without boiling, until sugar dissolves; bring to a boil. Boil, uncovered, without stirring, about 10 minutes or until caramel in colour. Pour toffee into prepared pan; top with sliced banana.

3 Combine eggs, oil, brown sugar and extract in medium bowl. Stir in sifted dry ingredients, then mashed banana; pour mixture into prepared pan. Bake, uncovered, in moderate oven about 40 minutes. Turn onto wire rack, peel off baking paper; turn cake top-side up. Serve cake warm or at room temperature with thick cream, if desired.

serves 8

VANILLA CHEESECAKE WITH POACHED QUINCES

PREPARATION TIME 20 MINUTES (PLUS REFRIGERATION TIME) **COOKING TIME** 2 HOURS 45 MINUTES

Granita biscuits are made from flour, wheat flakes, golden syrup, egg and malt, and their crumbly texture makes them perfectly suited to conversion into a cheesecake base.

125g Granita biscuits
80g butter, melted
1 vanilla bean
2 x 250g packets cream cheese, softened
2 eggs
½ cup (120g) sour cream
¼ cup (60ml) lemon juice
2²/₃ cups (590g) caster sugar
2 cups (500ml) water
2 medium quinces (660g),
  peeled, cored, quartered
2 strips lemon rind

1 Preheat oven to moderately slow. Insert base of 23cm springform tin upside down in tin to give a flat base; grease tin.

2 Blend or process biscuits until mixture resembles fine breadcrumbs. Add butter; process until combined. Using hand, press biscuit mixture evenly over base of prepared tin, cover; refrigerate about 30 minutes or until firm.

3 Meanwhile, split vanilla bean in half lengthways, scrape seeds into medium bowl; reserve pod for poached quinces. Add cheese, eggs, sour cream, juice and ²/₃ cup of the sugar to seeds; beat with electric mixer until smooth.

4 Place tin on oven tray; pour in cheesecake mixture. Bake, uncovered, in moderately slow oven about 35 minutes or until set. Turn oven off; cool cheesecake in oven with door ajar. Cover cheesecake; refrigerate overnight.

5 Meanwhile, stir the water and remaining sugar in medium saucepan over low heat until sugar dissolves. Add quince, rind and reserved vanilla pod; bring to a boil. Reduce heat; simmer, covered, about 2 hours or until quince is tender and rosy in colour. Cool quince in syrup, then slice thinly.

6 Return quince syrup to a boil. Reduce heat; simmer, uncovered, until syrup reduces by half; cool. Top cheesecake with quince slices; brush with syrup.

serves 12
tips Cheesecake and quince mixture may be made in advance and assembled close to serving.
Cheesecake without quince mixture may be frozen.

CREME BRULEE

PREPARATION TIME 15 MINUTES (PLUS REFRIGERATION TIME)
COOKING TIME 40 MINUTES

1 vanilla bean
3 cups (750ml) thickened cream
6 egg yolks
¼ cup (55g) caster sugar
¼ cup (40g) pure icing sugar

1 Preheat oven to moderate. Split vanilla bean in half lengthways; scrape seeds into medium heatproof bowl. Heat pod and cream in medium saucepan, without boiling.

2 Add egg yolks and caster sugar to seeds in bowl; gradually whisk in hot cream mixture. Place bowl over medium saucepan of simmering water; stir over heat about 10 minutes or until custard mixture thickens slightly and coats the back of a spoon. Discard pod.

3 Divide custard among six ½-cup (125ml) heatproof dishes. Place dishes in large baking dish; pour enough boiling water into baking dish to come halfway up sides of dishes. Bake, uncovered, in moderate oven about 20 minutes or until custards just set. Remove custards from water; cool to room temperature. Cover; refrigerate 3 hours or overnight.

4 Place custards in shallow flameproof dish filled with ice cubes; sprinkle custards evenly with sifted icing sugar. Using finger, distribute the sugar over the surface of each custard, pressing in gently; place under preheated hot grill until tops of crème brûlées are caramelised.

serves 6
tip You can also use a small blowtorch to melt then caramelise the icing sugar. Small blowtorches are available from hardware stores, some kitchenware shops and all professional cookware outlets.

CHOCOLATE BROWNIE WITH WARM·CHOCOLATE SAUCE

PREPARATION TIME 20 MINUTES **COOKING TIME** 30 MINUTES

150g butter, chopped
300g dark eating chocolate, chopped coarsely
1½ cups (330g) firmly packed brown sugar
4 eggs, beaten lightly
1 cup (150g) plain flour
½ cup (120g) sour cream
½ cup (75g) toasted hazelnuts, chopped coarsely

WARM CHOCOLATE SAUCE
150g dark eating chocolate, chopped coarsely
300ml thickened cream
⅓ cup (75g) firmly packed brown sugar
2 teaspoons coffee-flavoured liqueur

1 Preheat oven to moderate. Grease 20cm x 30cm lamington pan; line base and sides with baking paper.

2 Stir butter and chocolate in small saucepan over low heat until mixture is smooth. Transfer to medium bowl.

3 Stir in sugar and eggs, then flour, sour cream and nuts; spread mixture into prepared pan. Bake, uncovered, in moderate oven about 30 minutes. Cool in pan.

4 Meanwhile, make warm chocolate sauce.

5 Cut brownie into 16 pieces; serve drizzled with warm chocolate sauce.
WARM CHOCOLATE SAUCE Stir chocolate, cream and sugar in small saucepan over low heat until mixture is smooth. Remove from heat; stir in liqueur.

serves 8
tip We used Kahlúa for this recipe but you can use any coffee-flavoured liqueur you like.
serving suggestion Serve brownies with scoops of vanilla ice-cream.

RICH CHOCOLATE TART

PREPARATION TIME 25 MINUTES (PLUS REFRIGERATION TIME) **COOKING TIME** 55 MINUTES

This recipe can be made 1 day in advance.

4 egg yolks
2 eggs
¼ cup (55g) caster sugar
⅓ cup (80ml) thickened cream
300g dark eating chocolate, melted
1 teaspoon vanilla extract

PASTRY
1¼ cups (185g) plain flour
¼ cup (25g) cocoa powder
⅓ cup (55g) icing sugar mixture
150g cold butter, chopped
2 egg yolks
1 teaspoon iced water

1 Make pastry. Reduce oven temperature to moderately slow.
2 Beat egg yolks, eggs and caster sugar in small bowl with electric mixer until thick and creamy. Fold in cream, chocolate and extract.
3 Pour chocolate mixture into pastry case. Bake, uncovered, in moderately slow oven about 30 minutes or until filling is set. Cool 10 minutes. Serve tart dusted with a little extra sifted cocoa, if desired.
PASTRY Blend or process flour, sifted cocoa, sugar and butter until combined. Add egg yolks and the water; process until ingredients just come together. Knead dough on floured surface until smooth. Cover with plastic wrap; refrigerate 30 minutes. Preheat oven to moderate. Roll dough between sheets of baking paper until large enough to line base and side of greased 24cm-round loose-based flan tin. Ease dough into tin, press into side; trim edge. Cover; refrigerate 30 minutes. Cover pastry case with baking paper, fill with dried beans or rice; place on oven tray. Bake, uncovered, in moderate oven 15 minutes. Remove paper and beans; bake, uncovered, about 10 minutes or until browned lightly. Cool.

serves 10

RHUBARB AND ALMOND JALOUSIE

PREPARATION TIME 20 MINUTES **COOKING TIME** 40 MINUTES

You need approximately four large trimmed stalks of rhubarb for this recipe.

2 cups (250g) chopped rhubarb
⅓ cup (75g) caster sugar
2 sheets ready-rolled puff pastry
1 tablespoon apricot jam
1 egg white
1 tablespoon caster sugar, extra

FRANGIPANE FILLING
30g butter
¼ teaspoon vanilla extract
¼ cup (55g) caster sugar
1 egg
1 tablespoon plain flour
⅔ cup (80g) almond meal

1 Place rhubarb and sugar in medium saucepan; cook over low heat, stirring, until sugar dissolves and rhubarb softens.
2 Preheat oven to moderately hot. Grease oven tray.
3 Make frangipane filling.
4 Cut one pastry sheet into 14cm x 24cm rectangle; cut remaining pastry sheet into 16cm x 24cm rectangle. Leaving 2cm border around all sides, make about eight evenly spaced slits across width of larger pastry piece.
5 Place smaller pastry sheet on greased oven tray; spread with jam. Place filling on pastry, leaving 2cm border around the edges; top filling evenly with rhubarb mixture. Brush around border with egg white. Place remaining pastry sheet over filling; press edges of pastry together to seal.
6 Brush jalousie with remaining egg white; sprinkle with extra sugar. Bake, uncovered, in moderately hot oven about 35 minutes or until jalousie is browned lightly and cooked through. Serve warm or cool with vanilla ice-cream, if desired.
FRANGIPANE FILLING Beat butter, vanilla and sugar in small bowl with electric mixer until thick and creamy. Add egg; beat until combined. Stir in flour and almond meal.

serves 8

SAGO PLUM PUDDINGS WITH ORANGE CREAM

PREPARATION TIME 10 MINUTES (PLUS STANDING TIME) **COOKING TIME** 3 HOURS

Sago, also known as seed or pearl tapioca, comes from the sago palm and is used in soups and desserts, and as a thickening agent.

2 cups (500ml) water
²/₃ cup (130g) sago
1 teaspoon bicarbonate of soda
250g butter, softened
2 teaspoons vanilla extract
1 cup (220g) caster sugar
1 egg
½ cup (75g) plain flour
½ teaspoon bicarbonate of soda, extra
2 cups (140g) stale breadcrumbs
2 cups (320g) sultanas

ORANGE CREAM
2 teaspoons finely grated orange rind
1 tablespoon orange-flavoured liqueur
1 tablespoon icing sugar mixture
300ml thickened cream

1 Combine the water, sago and soda in medium bowl, cover; stand overnight.
2 Preheat oven to moderate. Grease eight ¾-cup (180ml) ovenproof moulds.
3 Beat butter, extract, sugar and egg in small bowl with electric mixer until light and fluffy. Stir in combined sifted flour and extra soda, sago mixture, breadcrumbs and sultanas.
4 Divide mixture among prepared moulds; cover tightly with foil. Place moulds in baking dish; pour enough boiling water into baking dish to come halfway up sides of moulds. Bake in moderate oven 3 hours, topping up water level with boiling water during cooking.
5 Meanwhile, make orange cream.
6 Turn puddings into serving bowls; serve dolloped with orange cream.
   ORANGE CREAM Beat ingredients in small bowl with electric mixer until soft peaks form.

serves 8
tip You can use Cointreau, Grand Marnier, Curaçao or any other orange-flavoured liqueur in this recipe.

VANILLA PEAR ALMOND CAKE

PREPARATION TIME 30 MINUTES (PLUS COOLING TIME) **COOKING TIME** 2 HOURS 15 MINUTES
Corellas are miniature dessert pears with pale flesh and a sweet, mild flavour.

8 corella pears (800g)
2½ cups (625ml) water
1 strip lemon rind
1¾ cups (385g) caster sugar
1 vanilla bean
125g butter, chopped
3 eggs
⅔ cup (160g) sour cream
⅔ cup (100g) plain flour
⅔ cup (100g) self-raising flour
¼ cup (40g) blanched almonds, toasted, chopped coarsely
40g dark eating chocolate, chopped coarsely
½ cup (60g) almond meal

1 Peel pears, leaving stems intact.
2 Combine the water, rind and 1 cup of the sugar in medium saucepan. Split vanilla bean in half lengthways; scrape seeds into saucepan, then place pod in saucepan. Stir over heat, without boiling, until sugar dissolves. Add pears; bring to a boil. Reduce heat; simmer, covered, about 30 minutes or until pears are just tender. Transfer pears to medium bowl; bring syrup to a boil. Boil, uncovered, until syrup reduces by half. Cool completely.
3 Preheat oven to moderately slow. Insert base of 23cm springform tin upside down in tin to give a flat base; grease tin.
4 Beat butter and remaining sugar in medium bowl with electric mixer until light and fluffy. Add eggs, one at a time, beating until just combined between additions. Add sour cream; beat until just combined. Mixture may curdle at this stage but will come together later. Stir in 2 tablespoons of the syrup, then flours, nuts, chocolate and almond meal.
5 Spread cake mixture into prepared tin; place pears upright around edge of tin, gently pushing to the bottom. Bake, uncovered, in moderately slow oven about 1 hour 35 minutes. Stand 10 minutes; remove from tin.
6 Serve cake warm, brushed with remaining syrup.

serves 8

CHOCOLATE SELF-SAUCING PUDDING

PREPARATION TIME 10 MINUTES **COOKING TIME** 40 MINUTES

1 cup (150g) self-raising flour
½ teaspoon bicarbonate of soda
½ cup (50g) cocoa powder
1¼ cups (275g) firmly packed brown sugar
80g butter, melted
½ cup (120g) sour cream
1 egg, beaten lightly
2 cups (500ml) boiling water

1 Preheat oven to moderate. Grease deep 1.5-litre (6-cup) ovenproof dish.
2 Sift flour, soda, half of the cocoa and ½ cup of the sugar into medium bowl; stir in combined butter, sour cream and egg.
3 Spread mixture into prepared dish. Sift remaining cocoa and remaining sugar evenly over mixture; gently pour over the boiling water. Bake, uncovered, in moderate oven about 40 minutes. Stand 5 minutes before serving.

serves 6
serving suggestion Serve with vanilla ice-cream, if desired.

GREEK CREAMED RICE

PREPARATION TIME 10 MINUTES **COOKING TIME** 40 MINUTES

1 litre (4 cups) milk
⅓ cup (75g) caster sugar
1 strip lemon rind
1 cinnamon stick
½ cup (100g) white
**   medium-grain rice**
2 teaspoons cornflour
2 teaspoons milk, extra
4 egg yolks
¼ cup (25g) toasted walnuts,
**   chopped coarsely**
1 teaspoon cinnamon sugar
1 tablespoon honey

1 Bring milk, sugar and rind to a boil in medium saucepan. Add cinnamon and rice; cook, covered, over low heat, stirring occasionally, about 30 minutes or until rice is tender. Discard rind and cinnamon stick.

2 Blend cornflour with extra milk in small bowl; stir in egg yolks. Stir egg mixture into rice mixture. Stir over heat until mixture boils and thickens.

3 Divide mixture among four ¾-cup (180ml) serving glasses; top with nuts, cinnamon sugar and honey.

serves 4

tips This recipe can be made a day ahead.
Creamed rice can be served warm or chilled.

PECAN PIE

PREPARATION TIME 25 MINUTES (PLUS REFRIGERATION TIME)
COOKING TIME 50 MINUTES

2 cups (280g) toasted pecans
6 egg yolks
½ cup (175g) golden syrup
½ cup (110g) firmly packed brown sugar
90g butter, melted
¼ cup (60ml) thickened cream

PASTRY

1¼ cups (185g) plain flour
⅓ cup (55g) icing sugar mixture
125g cold butter, chopped
1 egg yolk
1 teaspoon lemon juice

1 Grease 24cm-round loose-based flan tin. Make pastry.
2 Place nuts in pastry case. Combine egg yolks, syrup, sugar, butter and cream in small bowl; whisk until smooth. Pour mixture over nuts; bake, uncovered, in moderate oven about 30 minutes or until set. Cool. Serve with cream, if desired.

PASTRY Blend or process flour, icing sugar and butter until combined. Add yolk and juice; process until ingredients just come together. Knead dough on floured surface until smooth. Cover; refrigerate 30 minutes. Roll dough between sheets of baking paper until large enough to line prepared tin. Ease dough into tin, press into side; trim edge. Cover; refrigerate 30 minutes. Preheat oven to moderate. Place tin on oven tray. Line pastry case with baking paper, fill with dried beans or rice. Bake, uncovered, in moderate oven 15 minutes. Remove paper and beans; bake, uncovered, in moderate oven about 5 minutes or until browned lightly.

serves 8
tips This recipe can be made 1 day in advance. Uncooked rice or dried beans used to weigh down the pastry are not suitable for eating. Use them every time you bake blind; cool, then store in an airtight jar.

PLUM COBBLER

PREPARATION TIME 15 MINUTES **COOKING TIME** 40 MINUTES

825g can plums in syrup
¾ cup (110g) self-raising flour
¼ cup (55g) caster sugar
1 teaspoon ground cinnamon
60g butter, chopped
1 egg yolk
¼ cup (60ml) buttermilk, approximately
2 tablespoons coarsely chopped toasted hazelnuts
2 tablespoons icing sugar mixture

1 Preheat oven to moderate.

2 Drain plums over medium saucepan. Halve plums; discard stones. Add plums to pan; bring to a boil. Reduce heat; simmer, uncovered, about 5 minutes or until plums soften.

3 Strain plums; reserve ½ cup liquid. Place plums and reserved liquid in 1-litre (4-cup) ovenproof dish; place dish on oven tray.

4 Sift flour, caster sugar and cinnamon into medium bowl; rub in butter. Stir in egg yolk and enough of the buttermilk to make a soft, sticky dough. Drop heaped teaspoons of the mixture over hot plums; sprinkle with nuts.

5 Bake, uncovered, in moderate oven about 30 minutes or until browned lightly. Serve dusted with sifted icing sugar.

serves 4
tip Serve with cream or ice-cream, if desired.

GREEK-STYLE ALMOND BISCUITS

PREPARATION TIME 30 MINUTES   **COOKING TIME** 15 MINUTES

3 cups (375g) almond meal
1 cup (220g) caster sugar
¼ teaspoon almond essence
3 egg whites, beaten lightly
1 cup (80g) flaked almonds

1 Preheat oven to moderate. Grease two oven trays.
2 Combine almond meal, sugar and essence in large bowl. Add egg whites; stir until mixture forms a firm paste. Roll level tablespoons of the mixture through nuts; roll into 8cm logs. Shape logs to form crescents.
3 Place crescents on prepared trays; bake, uncovered, in moderate oven about 15 minutes or until browned lightly.

makes 25

STICKY DATE CAKE WITH BUTTERSCOTCH SAUCE

PREPARATION TIME 20 MINUTES **COOKING TIME** 55 MINUTES

3¾ cups (635g) dried pitted dates
3 cups (750ml) hot water
2 teaspoons bicarbonate of soda
185g butter, chopped
2¼ cups (500g) firmly packed brown sugar
6 eggs
3 cups (450g) self-raising flour
½ cup (60g) coarsely chopped walnuts
½ cup (60g) coarsely chopped pecans

BUTTERSCOTCH SAUCE

2 cups (440g) firmly packed brown sugar
500ml thickened cream
250g butter, chopped

1 Preheat oven to moderate. Grease 26cm x 36cm baking dish; double-line base and long sides with baking paper, bringing paper 5cm above edges of dish.

2 Combine dates and the water in medium saucepan; bring to a boil. Remove from heat; stir in soda. Stand 5 minutes. Blend or process date mixture until smooth.

3 Beat butter and sugar in large bowl with electric mixer until light and fluffy. Add eggs, one at a time, beating until combined between each addition. Stir in date mixture and flour; spread mixture into prepared dish, sprinkle with nuts. Bake, uncovered, in moderate oven about 50 minutes. Stand cake in dish 10 minutes; turn onto wire rack, turn cake top-side up.

4 Meanwhile, make butterscotch sauce.

5 Brush surface of hot cake with ⅓ cup of the hot butterscotch sauce. Serve with remaining sauce.
BUTTERSCOTCH SAUCE Stir ingredients in medium saucepan over heat, without boiling, until sugar dissolves; bring to a boil. Reduce heat; simmer 3 minutes.

serves 20
tips Cake is suitable to freeze. To defrost, wrap in foil and reheat in moderately slow oven for 20 minutes. Sauce is suitable to microwave.

SILKY CHOCOLATE MOUSSE

PREPARATION TIME 15 MINUTES (PLUS REFRIGERATION TIME) **COOKING TIME** 5 MINUTES

300g dark eating chocolate, chopped coarsely
50g unsalted butter
3 eggs, separated
1 tablespoon irish cream liqueur
¼ cup (55g) caster sugar
300ml thickened cream, whipped

1 Combine chocolate and butter in small saucepan; stir over low heat until smooth. Remove from heat.
2 Stir in egg yolks, one at a time, then liqueur; transfer mixture to large bowl. Cool.
3 Beat egg whites in small bowl with electric mixer until soft peaks form. Gradually add sugar, 1 tablespoon at a time, beating until sugar dissolves between additions.
4 Meanwhile, fold cream into chocolate mixture, then fold in egg white mixture, in two batches. Divide chocolate mousse among eight ½-cup (125ml) serving dishes. Cover; refrigerate 2 hours or until set.

serves 8
tips This recipe is best made 1 day ahead.
The chocolate and butter mixture is suitable to microwave.
We used Bailey's Irish Cream in this recipe, but you can use any irish cream liqueur.

GULAB JAMAN

PREPARATION TIME 20 MINUTES (PLUS STANDING TIME) **COOKING TIME** 15 MINUTES

A traditional Indian dessert, gulab jaman are deep-fried cream cheese dumplings saturated in a rosewater syrup.

2 cups (440g) caster sugar
2 cups (500ml) water
8 cardamom pods, bruised
2 cinnamon sticks
3 star anise
1 teaspoon rosewater
½ cup (75g) self-raising flour
**¼ cup (25g) full-cream
  milk powder**
**125g spreadable packaged
  cream cheese**
18 raisins
vegetable oil, for deep-frying

1 Stir sugar, the water, cardamom, cinnamon and star anise in medium saucepan over heat, without boiling, until sugar dissolves; bring to a boil. Boil, uncovered, without stirring, 5 minutes. Remove from heat; stir in rosewater. Cool.

2 Combine flour, milk powder and cheese in medium bowl; using wooden spoon, mix to a soft dough. Turn onto floured surface; knead about 10 minutes or until smooth. Roll 1 rounded teaspoon of the dough around each raisin.

3 Heat oil in wok, large saucepan or deep-fryer to 160°C; deep-fry balls, in batches, until golden brown. Add balls to rosewater syrup; stand gulab jaman 1 hour before serving.

makes 24

ITALIAN TRIFLE

PREPARATION TIME 30 MINUTES (PLUS REFRIGERATION AND STANDING TIMES) **COOKING TIME** 5 MINUTES

This recipe is best when prepared a day ahead and refrigerated overnight; stand at room temperature for half an hour before serving. Limoncello is an Italian lemon liqueur that is also fabulous served chilled with this trifle. If it is unavailable, substitute an orange-flavoured liqueur or use 1 tablespoon finely grated lemon rind. Candied figs are usually sold at health food shops and specialty cheese counters, however you can use glacé figs, if you prefer.

¼ cup (60ml) water
½ cup (125ml) lemon juice
1¼ cups (275g) caster sugar
⅓ cup (80ml) limoncello
1 cup (200g) ricotta
1 cup (250g) mascarpone
½ cup (150g) candied figs, chopped coarsely
¾ cup (110g) toasted hazelnuts,
  chopped coarsely
100g dark eating chocolate, chopped coarsely
100g dark eating chocolate, melted
600ml thickened cream
250g packet savoiardi sponge finger biscuits

1 Stir the water, juice and ¾ cup of the sugar in medium saucepan over heat, without boiling, until sugar dissolves; bring to a boil. Boil, uncovered, without stirring, about 2 minutes or until syrup thickens slightly. Stir in liqueur off the heat; cool completely.

2 Meanwhile, beat ricotta and remaining sugar in large bowl until smooth. Add mascarpone; beat until just combined. Fold in figs, nuts and chopped chocolate. Place half of the ricotta mixture in medium bowl; fold in melted chocolate.

3 Beat cream in medium bowl with electric mixer until soft peaks form; fold half of the cream into each of the ricotta mixtures.

4 Pour half of the lemon syrup into shallow medium bowl; soak half of the biscuits until just softened. Line deep 3-litre (12-cup) rectangular serving dish with soaked biscuits. Spread half of the chocolate ricotta mixture then half of the plain ricotta mixture over biscuits. Repeat process with remaining syrup, biscuits and ricotta mixtures. Cover; refrigerate overnight. Stand at room temperature for half an hour. Serve dusted with cocoa powder, if desired.

serves 10

PEAR CHARLOTTES WITH FIG SYRUP

PREPARATION TIME 20 MINUTES **COOKING TIME** 45 MINUTES

5 large pears (1.8kg)
1 cup (220g) firmly packed brown sugar
1 cinnamon stick
1 cup (250ml) water
16 slices day-old white bread
90g butter, melted
4 dried figs, sliced thinly
¼ cup (60ml) brandy

1 Preheat oven to moderately hot. Grease four 1-cup (250ml) ovenproof dishes.

2 Peel and core pears; chop coarsely. Place pear in medium saucepan with sugar, cinnamon and the water; bring to a boil. Reduce heat; simmer, uncovered, about 10 minutes or until pears are tender. Strain pears over medium bowl; reserve syrup and cinnamon.

3 Cut eight 8.5cm rounds from eight bread slices. Remove crusts from remaining bread slices; cut each slice into three 3cm-wide strips. Halve each strip crossways.

4 Combine butter and 2 tablespoons of the syrup in small bowl; brush butter mixture on one side of all bread pieces. Place one bread round, buttered-side down, in each dish; line side of each dish with bread fingers, buttered-side against dish, overlapping slightly. Fill centres with pear; top with remaining bread rounds, buttered-side up. Bake, uncovered, in moderately hot oven about 30 minutes or until browned lightly.

5 Meanwhile, bring 1 cup of the reserved syrup and cinnamon to a boil in small saucepan; add figs. Reduce heat; simmer, uncovered, about 5 minutes or until syrup reduces by half. Add brandy; simmer, uncovered, 3 minutes.

6 Turn charlottes onto serving plates; spoon fig mixture over each charlotte.

serves 4

tip You can replace pears with apples or quinces, if you prefer.

RHUBARB AND PEAR SPONGE PUDDING

PREPARATION TIME 15 MINUTES **COOKING TIME** 50 MINUTES

825g can pear slices in natural juice
800g rhubarb, trimmed, cut into 4cm pieces
2 tablespoons caster sugar
2 eggs
1/3 cup (75g) caster sugar, extra
2 tablespoons plain flour
2 tablespoons self-raising flour
2 tablespoons cornflour

1 Preheat oven to moderate.
2 Drain pears; reserve ¾ cup (180ml) of the juice. Combine reserved juice, rhubarb and sugar in large saucepan; cook, stirring occasionally, about 5 minutes or until rhubarb is just tender. Stir in pears. Pour mixture into deep 1.75-litre (7-cup) ovenproof dish.
3 Meanwhile, beat eggs in small bowl with electric mixer until thick and creamy. Gradually add extra sugar, 1 tablespoon at a time, beating until sugar dissolves between additions. Gently fold in combined sifted flours.
4 Spread sponge mixture over hot rhubarb mixture. Bake, uncovered, in moderate oven about 45 minutes or until browned lightly and cooked through.

serves 6
tip Rhubarb mixture is suitable to microwave.

SOUR CHERRY CHOCOLATE CHEESECAKE

PREPARATION TIME 40 MINUTES (PLUS REFRIGERATION AND STANDING TIMES)
COOKING TIME 1 HOUR 10 MINUTES (PLUS COOLING TIME)

250g plain sweet biscuits
125g butter, melted
680g jar morello cherries
3 x 250g packets cream cheese, softened
3 eggs
¾ cup (180g) sour cream
¼ cup (60ml) lemon juice
1¾ cups (385g) caster sugar
50g dark eating chocolate, melted
¼ cup (25g) cocoa powder

1 Preheat oven to slow. Grease 22cm springform tin.
2 Blend or process biscuits until mixture resembles fine breadcrumbs. Add butter; process until combined.
3 Using one hand, press biscuit mixture evenly over base and 5cm up the side of prepared tin, place on oven tray; refrigerate about 30 minutes or until firm.
4 Meanwhile, drain cherries over small bowl; reserve 1 cup of the juice. Beat cheese, eggs, sour cream, lemon juice and 1 cup of the sugar in large bowl with electric mixer until smooth. Place half of the cheese mixture in medium bowl; stir in chocolate and sifted cocoa.
5 Pour plain and chocolate mixtures alternately into tin; pull a skewer backwards and forwards through mixture for a marbled effect; top with ½ cup of the cherries. Bake, uncovered, in slow oven about 1 hour or until set. Turn oven off; cool cheesecake in oven with door ajar. Cover; refrigerate several hours or overnight. Stand cheesecake at room temperature 30 minutes before serving.
6 Meanwhile, stir reserved cherry juice with remaining sugar in small saucepan over heat until sugar dissolves; bring to a boil. Boil, uncovered, without stirring, 5 minutes. Stir in remaining cherries. Transfer to medium heatproof jug; cool 10 minutes. Serve cheesecake with cherry sauce.

serves 12
tip When cutting cheesecake, dip the knife in hot water to ensure a clean cut.

ROASTED PEAR TART

PREPARATION TIME 10 MINUTES
COOKING TIME 20 MINUTES

1 sheet ready-rolled puff pastry
1 egg, beaten lightly
825g can pear halves in natural juice, drained
1 tablespoon pure maple syrup
30g butter, melted

1 Preheat oven to moderately hot. Grease oven tray.
2 Cut pastry sheet in half; place pastry halves about 2cm apart on prepared tray, brush with egg.
3 Place three pear halves, cut-side down, on each pastry half; brush pears with combined syrup and butter. Bake, uncovered, in moderately hot oven about 20 minutes or until pastry is puffed and browned lightly.

serves 4
tip Dust tart with icing sugar and serve with cream or ice-cream, if desired.

TOFFEED MANDARINS WITH ICE-CREAM

PREPARATION TIME 10 MINUTES
COOKING TIME 10 MINUTES

50g butter
$1/3$ cup (75g) firmly packed brown sugar
5 medium mandarins (1kg), peeled, segmented
1 litre (4 cups) vanilla ice-cream

1 Melt butter in large frying pan; cook sugar and mandarins, stirring, until sugar dissolves and mandarins soften slightly.
2 Divide ice-cream among serving bowls; top with warm mandarin mixture.

serves 4
serving suggestion Serve with almond bread.

PLUMS WITH
SOUR CREAM

PREPARATION TIME 5 MINUTES
COOKING TIME 5 MINUTES

825g can plums in syrup, drained
½ cup (120g) sour cream
½ cup (140g) honey-flavoured yogurt
⅓ cup (75g) firmly packed brown sugar

1 Halve plums; discard stones. Divide plums among four
   1-cup (250ml) shallow flameproof serving dishes.
2 Combine sour cream, yogurt and 2 tablespoons of
   the sugar in small bowl. Spoon sour cream mixture
   over plums; sprinkle with remaining sugar. Place
   under preheated grill about 3 minutes or until sugar
   dissolves.

serves 4

TOBLERONE FONDUE

PREPARATION TIME 5 MINUTES
COOKING TIME 5 MINUTES

200g Toblerone, chopped coarsely
½ cup (125ml) thickened cream
1 tablespoon coffee-flavoured liqueur

1 Stir Toblerone and cream in small saucepan until
   smooth. Remove from heat; stir in liqueur. Transfer
   fondue to serving bowl.
2 Place fondue in centre of dining table; serve with
   fresh fruit and biscotti.

serves 6
tip We used Kahlúa for this recipe but you can use
any coffee-flavoured liqueur you like.

VANILLA PANNA COTTA WITH BERRY JELLY

PREPARATION TIME 20 MINUTES (PLUS REFRIGERATION TIME) **COOKING TIME** 15 MINUTES

120g raspberries
½ teaspoon gelatine
1½ tablespoons caster sugar
1 tablespoon lemon juice
⅓ cup (80ml) cranberry juice

VANILLA PANNA COTTA

2 teaspoons gelatine
¼ cup (55g) caster sugar
⅔ cup (160ml) milk
300ml thickened cream
½ teaspoon vanilla extract

1 Grease four ⅔-cup (160ml) metal moulds. Place four raspberries in each mould; reserve remaining raspberries.

2 Sprinkle gelatine and sugar over combined juices in small heatproof jug; stand jug in small saucepan of simmering water, stirring until gelatine and sugar dissolve.

3 Divide gelatine mixture among prepared moulds, cover; refrigerate about 2 hours or until set.

4 Meanwhile, make vanilla panna cotta. Gently pour cooled panna cotta into moulds, cover; refrigerate 3 hours or overnight.

5 Turn panna cotta onto serving plates; serve with remaining raspberries.
   VANILLA PANNA COTTA Sprinkle gelatine and sugar over combined milk and cream in small saucepan. Stir over low heat, without boiling, until gelatine and sugar dissolve; add extract. Strain into medium jug; cool to room temperature.

serves 4

MANGO BOMBE ALASKA

PREPARATION TIME 20 MINUTES (PLUS FREEZING TIME) **COOKING TIME** 5 MINUTES

2 litres mango ice-cream, softened
¼ cup (60ml) orange juice
2 tablespoons orange-flavoured liqueur
16cm-round unfilled packaged sponge cake
1 large mango (600g), sliced thinly
4 egg whites
1 cup (220g) caster sugar

1 Line 15cm 1.375-litre (5½-cup) pudding basin or bowl with plastic wrap, extending plastic 5cm over edge of basin.
2 Pack ice-cream into prepared basin, cover with foil; freeze about 2 hours or until firm.
3 Preheat oven to very hot.
4 Combine juice and liqueur in small jug. Trim top of cake to flatten; split cake in half horizontally through centre. Place bottom layer of cake on oven tray; brush with half of the juice mixture. Top with mango, then with remaining cake half; brush with remaining juice mixture.
5 Invert ice-cream from basin onto cake; working quickly, trim cake to exact size of ice-cream. Return to freezer.
6 Beat egg whites in small bowl with electric mixer until soft peaks form; gradually add sugar, beating until sugar dissolves between additions.
7 Remove bombe from freezer; spread meringue over to enclose bombe completely. Bake, uncovered, in very hot oven about 3 minutes or until browned lightly. Lift onto serving plate; serve immediately.

serves 6
tips If mango ice-cream is unavailable, place canned drained mango slices and scoops of vanilla ice-cream alternately in the pudding basin.
You can use Cointreau, Grand Marnier, Curaçao or any other orange-flavoured liqueur in this recipe.

PEACH AND RASPBERRY TRIFLE

PREPARATION TIME 30 MINUTES (PLUS REFRIGERATION TIME)
COOKING TIME 10 MINUTES

85g packet raspberry jelly crystals
250g unfilled packaged sponge cake
2 tablespoons raspberry jam
½ cup (125ml) sweet sherry
¼ cup (30g) custard powder
¼ cup (55g) caster sugar
1½ cups (375ml) milk
½ teaspoon vanilla extract
300ml thickened cream
825g can sliced peaches, drained
2 tablespoons flaked almonds, toasted

1 Make jelly according to directions on packet, cover; refrigerate until
   mixture is the consistency of unbeaten egg white.
2 Meanwhile, split cake in half horizontally through centre; sandwich cake
   halves with jam. Cut cake into 3cm squares.
3 Place cake in 2.5-litre (10-cup) deep serving bowl; sprinkle with sherry.
4 Combine custard powder and sugar in medium saucepan. Gradually blend
   in milk; stir over heat until mixture boils and thickens. Remove from heat,
   stir in extract and ½ cup of the cream. Cover surface completely with
   plastic wrap; cool to room temperature.
5 Meanwhile, pour jelly over cake, cover; refrigerate until jelly sets.
6 Top jelly with peaches, then with custard.
7 Beat remaining cream in small bowl with electric mixer until soft peaks
   form. Spread cream over custard; refrigerate 2 hours or overnight. Sprinkle
   with nuts just before serving.

serves 10
tips This recipe can be made a day in advance.
The custard can be prepared in a microwave oven.

STRAWBERRIES AND CREAM POWDER PUFFS

PREPARATION TIME 25 MINUTES **COOKING TIME** 10 MINUTES

2 eggs
$1/3$ cup (75g) caster sugar
2 tablespoons cornflour
2 tablespoons plain flour
2 tablespoons self-raising flour
$2/3$ cup (160ml) thickened cream
$1/3$ cup (55g) icing sugar mixture
250g strawberries, chopped coarsely

1 Preheat oven to moderate. Grease and flour two 12-hole shallow patty pans.
2 Beat eggs in small bowl with electric mixer until thick and creamy. Gradually add caster sugar, 1 tablespoon at a time, beating until sugar dissolves between additions. Sift flours together three times onto baking paper; fold into egg mixture.
3 Divide mixture among prepared pans. Bake, uncovered, in moderate oven about 8 minutes. Turn immediately onto wire rack to cool.
4 Beat cream and half of the icing sugar in small bowl with electric mixer until soft peaks form; fold in strawberries. Divide cream mixture among half of the sponges; top with remaining sponges. Serve powder puffs dusted with remaining icing sugar.

makes 12
tip The sponges should be baked on the day you intend to serve them, then assembled with berries and cream just before serving.

MANGO-PASSIONFRUIT SORBET WITH GRILLED MANGO

PREPARATION TIME 30 MINUTES (PLUS FREEZING TIME) **COOKING TIME** 25 MINUTES
You need about six passionfruit for this recipe.

½ cup (125ml) passionfruit pulp
1 cup (250ml) water
½ cup (110g) caster sugar
1 large mango (600g), chopped coarsely
2 tablespoons orange-flavoured liqueur
3 egg whites
4 small mangoes (1.2kg)
2 tablespoons brown sugar
1 lime, cut into 8 wedges

1 Strain passionfruit pulp over small jug; reserve seeds.
2 Stir the water and caster sugar in small saucepan over heat, without boiling, until sugar dissolves; bring to a boil. Reduce heat; simmer, uncovered, without stirring, about 10 minutes or until mixture thickens. Cool.
3 Blend or process chopped mango until smooth; transfer to small bowl. Stir in pulp, syrup and liqueur. Pour mixture into 14cm x 21cm loaf pan, cover with foil; freeze about 3 hours or until just firm.
4 Process sorbet with egg whites until almost smooth. Stir in 2 tablespoons reserved passionfruit seeds; discard remaining seeds. Return sorbet to pan, cover; freeze overnight.
5 Just before serving, slice cheeks from small mangoes; score each cheek in shallow criss-cross pattern, taking care not to cut through skin. Sprinkle brown sugar over cheeks; place under hot grill until browned lightly. Serve sorbet with mango cheeks and lime wedges.

serves 4
tip You can use Cointreau, Grand Marnier, Curaçao or any other orange-flavoured liqueur in this recipe.

MANGO AND LEMON CHIFFON TRIFLE

PREPARATION TIME 30 MINUTES (PLUS REFRIGERATION TIME) **COOKING TIME** 5 MINUTES

200g unfilled packaged sponge cake
85g packet mango jelly crystals
1 large mango (600g), sliced thinly

LEMON CHIFFON

2 eggs, separated
2 egg yolks
½ cup (110g) caster sugar
1 teaspoon finely grated lemon rind
1 teaspoon gelatine
¼ cup (60ml) water
1 tablespoon lemon juice
¾ cup (180ml) thickened cream, whipped

1 Cut sponge into 1cm squares; divide among six 2-cup (500ml) serving glasses.

2 Make jelly according to directions on packet. Pour half of the warm jelly mixture over sponge, cover; refrigerate until set. Cover remaining jelly, refrigerate until the consistency of unbeaten egg white.

3 Meanwhile, make lemon chiffon.

4 Reserve six slices of the mango. Blend or process remaining mango until smooth. Spoon soft jelly over sponge; top with mango puree. Spoon lemon chiffon over puree; refrigerate until set. Top each trifle with one of the reserved mango slices.

LEMON CHIFFON Beat all egg yolks, half of the sugar and the rind in small bowl with electric mixer until thick and creamy. Sprinkle gelatine over the water in small heatproof jug; stand jug in small saucepan of simmering water. Stir until gelatine dissolves; add juice, stir into egg mixture. Transfer to large bowl. Beat egg whites in small bowl with electric mixer until soft peaks form. Gradually add remaining sugar, 1 tablespoon at a time, beating until sugar dissolves between additions; fold into lemon mixture, then fold in cream.

serves 6

PROFITEROLES WITH CHOCOLATE LIQUEUR SAUCE

PREPARATION TIME 45 MINUTES
(PLUS REFRIGERATION TIME)

COOKING TIME 35 MINUTES

Choux is different from other pastries because it's made by melting butter in water, then beating in the flour over heat. The glossy, thick, paste-like dough is often piped into the required shape before baking.

CHOUX PASTRY

75g butter
¾ cup (180ml) water
¾ cup (110g) plain flour
3 eggs

CREME PATISSIERE

2¼ cups (560ml) milk
1 vanilla bean, split
6 egg yolks
⅔ cup (150g) caster sugar
½ cup (75g) plain flour

CHOCOLATE LIQUEUR SAUCE

**100g dark eating chocolate,
 chopped coarsely**
30g butter
⅓ cup (80ml) cream
**1 tablespoon orange-flavoured
 liqueur**

1 Make choux pastry.

2 Meanwhile, make crème pâtissière and chocolate liqueur sauce.

3 Spoon crème pâtissière into piping bag fitted with 1cm plain tube; pipe cream through cuts into profiteroles. Serve profiteroles drizzled with chocolate liqueur sauce.

CHOUX PASTRY Preheat oven to moderately hot. Lightly grease two oven trays. Combine butter with the water in medium saucepan; bring to a boil. Add flour; beat with wooden spoon over heat until mixture comes away from base and side of saucepan and forms a smooth ball. Transfer mixture to small bowl; beat in eggs, one at a time, with electric mixer until mixture becomes glossy. Drop rounded teaspoons of choux pastry dough 4cm apart on prepared trays; bake, uncovered, in moderately hot oven about 7 minutes or until pastries puff. Reduce oven temperature to moderate; bake, uncovered, about 10 minutes or until browned lightly and crisp. Cut small opening in side of each profiterole; bake, uncovered, in moderate oven about 5 minutes or until profiteroles dry out. Cool to room temperature before filling with crème pâtissière.

CREME PATISSIERE Bring milk and vanilla bean to a boil in medium saucepan; remove from heat. Stand 10 minutes; discard vanilla bean. Meanwhile, beat egg yolks and sugar in medium bowl with electric mixer until thick; beat in sifted flour. With motor operating on low speed, gradually beat in hot milk mixture. Return custard mixture to same saucepan; stir over heat until mixture boils and thickens. Reduce heat; simmer, stirring, 2 minutes. Remove from heat; transfer to medium bowl. Cover surface with plastic wrap to prevent skin forming; refrigerate until cold.

CHOCOLATE LIQUEUR SAUCE Stir chocolate, butter and cream in small saucepan over low heat until smooth. Stir in liqueur.

makes 36

tips Chocolate liqueur sauce can be made in a microwave oven. You can use Cointreau, Grand Marnier, Curaçao or any other orange-flavoured liqueur in this recipe.

Beat until mixture comes away from side of pan and forms a smooth ball.

Beat in eggs until pastry mixture drops from the beaters in a V-shape.

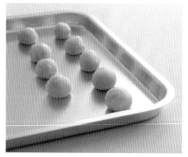

Place balls of choux pastry dough on greased oven trays about 4cm apart.

BERRY CUSTARD PASTRIES

PREPARATION TIME 40 MINUTES **COOKING TIME** 12 MINUTES

2 sheets ready-rolled butter puff pastry
2 tablespoons icing sugar mixture
700g mixed fresh berries

CUSTARD CREAM
300ml thickened cream
300g thick vanilla custard
¼ cup (40g) icing sugar mixture

1 Preheat oven to hot. Grease and line three oven trays with baking paper.
2 Cut one pastry sheet in half. Sprinkle one half with 2 teaspoons of the sugar; place remaining half of the pastry on top. Roll pastry up tightly from short side; cut log into eight rounds. Repeat with remaining pastry sheet and another 2 teaspoons of the sugar.
3 Place rounds, cut-side up, on board dusted lightly with icing sugar; roll each round into an oval about 8cm x 10cm.
4 Place ovals on prepared trays. Bake, uncovered, in hot oven about 12 minutes or until pastries are browned lightly and crisp, turning halfway through baking.
5 Meanwhile, make custard cream.
6 Place a drop of the custard cream on each of eight serving plates (to stop pastry sliding); top each with a pastry. Divide half of the berries over pastries, then top with custard cream, remaining berries and remaining pastries. Dust with sifted remaining sugar.
CUSTARD CREAM Beat cream, custard and sugar in small bowl with electric mixer until soft peaks form. Cover; refrigerate 30 minutes or until firm.

serves 8
tips This recipe can be prepared a day ahead, then assembled just before serving. Keep pastries in an airtight container and the custard cream, covered, under refrigeration.
We used a mixture of fresh berries that included mulberries, strawberries, youngberries and blueberries.

PEACH AND RASPBERRY MERINGUE ROLL

PREPARATION TIME 25 MINUTES **COOKING TIME** 20 MINUTES

4 egg whites
¾ cup (165g) caster sugar
1 teaspoon cornflour
1 teaspoon white vinegar
⅓ cup (25g) flaked almonds
3 medium peaches (450g)
300ml thickened cream
1 tablespoon peach schnapps
120g raspberries

1 Preheat oven to moderate. Grease 25cm x 30cm swiss roll pan; line base and long sides with baking paper, extending paper 5cm over edges.

2 Beat egg whites in small bowl with electric mixer until soft peaks form. Gradually add sugar, 1 tablespoon at a time, beating until sugar dissolves between additions. Fold in cornflour and vinegar.

3 Spread mixture into prepared pan; sprinkle with almonds. Bake, uncovered, in moderate oven about 20 minutes or until meringue is browned lightly.

4 Cover wire rack with baking paper. Turn meringue onto paper; peel away lining paper. Cool.

5 Meanwhile, cut small cross in stem end of each peach; place in medium heatproof bowl. Cover with boiling water; stand 30 seconds, drain. Peel skin from peaches; slice flesh thinly.

6 Beat cream and schnapps in small bowl with electric mixer until soft peaks form; spread evenly over meringue. Top with peach and raspberries. Roll meringue firmly, from long side, by lifting paper and using it to guide roll into shape.

serves 8
tip You can replace peach schnapps with peach liqueur or brandy, if desired.

WHITE CHOCOLATE AND STRAWBERRY CHEESECAKE

PREPARATION TIME 25 MINUTES (PLUS REFRIGERATION TIME) **COOKING TIME** 5 MINUTES

Butternut Snap biscuits, containing rolled oats, coconut and golden syrup, resemble anzac biscuits and can be found at your local supermarket.

185g Butternut Snap biscuits
80g butter, melted
3 teaspoons gelatine
2 tablespoons water
2 x 250g packets cream cheese, softened
400g can sweetened condensed milk
300ml thickened cream
150g white eating chocolate, melted
500g large strawberries, halved
¼ cup (80g) strawberry jam, warmed, strained
1 tablespoon lemon juice

1 Grease 23cm springform tin.
2 Blend or process biscuits until mixture resembles fine breadcrumbs. Add butter; process until combined. Using hand, press biscuit mixture evenly over base of prepared tin, cover; refrigerate about 30 minutes or until firm.
3 Sprinkle gelatine over the water in small heatproof jug; stand jug in small saucepan of simmering water. Stir until gelatine dissolves. Cool 5 minutes.
4 Meanwhile, beat cheese and condensed milk in medium bowl with electric mixer until smooth. Beat cream in small bowl with electric mixer until soft peaks form.
5 Stir warm gelatine mixture into cheese mixture; fold in cream and chocolate. Pour cheesecake mixture into prepared tin, spreading evenly over biscuit base. Cover; refrigerate overnight.
6 Arrange strawberries on top of cheesecake; brush strawberries with combined jam and juice.

serves 10

CHOCOLATE ESPRESSO MOUSSE CAKE

PREPARATION TIME 40 MINUTES (PLUS REFRIGERATION TIME) **COOKING TIME** 15 MINUTES

6 eggs, separated
½ cup (80g) icing sugar mixture
¼ cup (25g) cocoa powder
2 tablespoons cornflour
150g dark eating chocolate, melted
1 tablespoon water
1 tablespoon instant coffee powder
1 tablespoon hot water
3 cups (750ml) thickened cream
450g dark eating chocolate, melted, extra
2 teaspoons cocoa powder, extra

1 Preheat oven to moderate. Grease 25cm x 30cm swiss roll pan; line base and two long sides with baking paper.
2 Beat egg yolks and sugar in small bowl with electric mixer until thick and creamy; transfer mixture to large bowl. Fold in combined sifted cocoa and cornflour, then chocolate and the water.
3 Beat egg whites in small bowl with electric mixer until soft peaks form. Fold egg whites, in two batches, into chocolate mixture. Spread mixture into prepared pan; bake, uncovered, in moderate oven about 15 minutes. Turn cake onto baking-paper-lined wire rack to cool.
4 Grease 23cm springform tin; line side with baking paper, extending paper 5cm above edge of tin. Cut 23cm-diameter circle from cooled cake; place in prepared tin. Discard remaining cake.
5 Dissolve coffee in the hot water in small jug; cool. Beat cream and coffee mixture in medium bowl with electric mixer until soft peaks form. Fold in cooled extra chocolate.
6 Pour coffee mixture over cake in tin, cover; refrigerate about 3 hours or until set.
7 Transfer cake from tin to serving plate; dust with sifted extra cocoa.

serves 12

ROAST NECTARINE TART

PREPARATION TIME 40 MINUTES (PLUS REFRIGERATION TIME) **COOKING TIME** 45 MINUTES

8 nectarines (1.5kg), halved, stone removed
¼ cup (60ml) orange juice
½ cup (110g) firmly packed brown sugar

PASTRY
1⅔ cups (250g) plain flour
⅔ cup (110g) icing sugar mixture
125g cold butter, chopped
1 egg yolk
1½ tablespoons cold water, approximately

CREME PATISSIERE
300ml thickened cream
1 cup (250ml) milk
½ cup (110g) caster sugar
1 vanilla bean
3 egg yolks
2 tablespoons cornflour
90g unsalted butter, chopped

1 Grease 19cm x 27cm loose-based flan tin. Make pastry.
2 Make crème pâtissière while pastry case is cooling.
3 Increase oven temperature to hot. Place nectarines, in single layer, in large shallow baking dish; sprinkle with juice and sugar. Roast, uncovered, in hot oven about 20 minutes or until nectarines are soft. Cool.
4 Meanwhile, spoon crème pâtissière into pastry case, cover; refrigerate about 30 minutes or until firm. Top with nectarines.

PASTRY Blend or process flour, sugar and butter until combined. Add egg yolk and enough of the water to make ingredients just come together. Knead dough on floured surface until smooth. Cover; refrigerate 30 minutes. Preheat oven to moderate. Roll dough between sheets of baking paper until large enough to line prepared tin. Ease dough into prepared tin, press into sides; trim edges. Cover; refrigerate 30 minutes. Cover pastry case with baking paper, fill with dried beans or rice; place on oven tray. Bake, uncovered, in moderate oven 10 minutes. Remove paper and beans; bake, uncovered, in moderate oven about 10 minutes or until pastry case is browned lightly. Cool.

CREME PATISSIERE Combine cream, milk and sugar in medium saucepan. Split vanilla bean in half lengthways, scrape seeds into saucepan, then add pod; bring to a boil. Remove from heat; discard pod. Beat egg yolks in small bowl with electric mixer until thick and creamy; beat in cornflour. Gradually beat in hot cream mixture. Strain mixture into same cleaned saucepan; stir over heat until mixture boils and thickens. Remove from heat; whisk in butter. Cover surface of custard with plastic wrap; cool to room temperature.

serves 8

tip Uncooked rice or dried beans used to weigh down the pastry are not suitable for eating. Use them every time you bake blind; store in an airtight storage jar.

WHITE CHOCOLATE FROZEN CHRISTMAS PUDDING

PREPARATION TIME 25 MINUTES (PLUS STANDING AND FREEZING TIMES)
Craisins are dried cranberries and are sold in most supermarkets.

½ cup (75g) craisins
½ cup (115g) finely chopped
    glacé pineapple
¼ cup (60ml) brandy
2 litres vanilla ice-cream,
    softened
2 cups (280g) vienna almonds,
    chopped coarsely
360g white eating chocolate,
    melted

1 Line 17.5cm 1.75-litre (7-cup) pudding basin with plastic wrap, extending plastic 5cm over edge of basin.
2 Combine fruit and brandy in large bowl; stand 30 minutes.
3 Stir ice-cream and nuts into fruit mixture until combined. Pack ice-cream mixture into prepared basin, cover with foil; freeze overnight.
4 Turn pudding onto tray; remove plastic wrap, return pudding to freezer.
5 Cut a piece of paper into 35cm circle to use as a guide. Cover paper with a large sheet of plastic wrap. Spread chocolate over plastic wrap. Quickly drape plastic, chocolate-side down, over pudding. Smooth pudding with hands before gently peeling away plastic wrap. Trim base; centre pudding on serving plate.

serves 12
tips Decorate pudding with frozen cherries and dust with icing sugar just before serving, if desired.
This recipe can be made 1 week ahead. Add chocolate coating up to 3 hours before serving.

Using paper circle as a guide, spread the chocolate over the plastic wrap.

Carefully drape the plastic wrap, chocolate-side down, over pudding.

Smooth pudding with hands before gently peeling away the plastic wrap.

BAKED PLUMS WITH FROZEN ALMOND CREAM

PREPARATION TIME 20 MINUTES (PLUS FREEZING TIME) **COOKING TIME** 30 MINUTES
Frozen almond cream is best made a day ahead.

16 ripe medium plums (1.8kg)
1 vanilla bean
½ cup (125ml) dry red wine
½ cup (110g) caster sugar

FROZEN ALMOND CREAM
600ml thickened cream
¼ cup (40g) icing sugar mixture
½ teaspoon vanilla extract
150g almond nougat, chopped finely
½ cup (80g) toasted almonds, chopped finely

1 Make frozen almond cream.
2 Preheat oven to moderate.
3 Cut shallow cross in base of each plum; place plums, cut-side up, in single layer, in large shallow baking dish. Split vanilla bean in half lengthways; add to dish.
4 Pour wine over plums; sprinkle plums with sugar. Bake, uncovered, in moderate oven about 30 minutes or until plums are tender, brushing plums with juices halfway through cooking time. Discard vanilla bean.
5 Meanwhile, stand frozen almond cream at room temperature for 10 minutes.
6 Serve plums with frozen almond cream.
   FROZEN ALMOND CREAM Line 14cm x 21cm loaf pan with plastic wrap. Beat cream, sugar and extract in small bowl with electric mixer until soft peaks form; gently fold in nougat and nuts. Spread mixture into prepared pan, cover with foil; freeze overnight.

serves 8
tip Separate pieces of nougat before folding into cream mixture to prevent them from clumping together.

WENDY'S SPONGE CAKE

PREPARATION TIME 20 MINUTES   **COOKING TIME** 20 MINUTES

4 eggs
¾ cup (165g) caster sugar
⅔ cup (100g) wheaten cornflour
¼ cup (30g) custard powder
1 teaspoon cream of tartar
½ teaspoon bicarbonate of soda
300ml thickened cream
1 tablespoon icing sugar mixture
½ teaspoon vanilla extract
¼ cup (80g) strawberry jam, warmed
250g strawberries, sliced thinly
1 tablespoon icing sugar mixture, extra

1 Preheat oven to moderate. Grease and flour two deep
22cm-round cake pans.
2 Beat eggs and caster sugar in small bowl with electric mixer about
5 minutes or until thick and creamy; transfer to large bowl.
3 Sift dry ingredients twice onto paper, then sift over egg mixture;
gently fold ingredients together.
4 Divide mixture evenly between prepared pans; bake, uncovered, in
moderate oven about 20 minutes. Turn sponges immediately onto
baking-paper-lined wire rack; turn top-side up to cool.
5 Beat cream, icing sugar and extract in small bowl with electric mixer
until firm peaks form. Place one sponge on serving plate; spread first
with jam, then with cream mixture. Top with strawberry slices, then
with remaining sponge. Dust with sifted extra icing sugar mixture.

serves 10
tip When folding flour into egg mixture, you can use a large metal
spoon, a rubber spatula or a whisk, or use one hand like a rake.

ITALIAN RICOTTA CHEESECAKE

PREPARATION TIME 30 MINUTES (PLUS REFRIGERATION TIME)   **COOKING TIME** 1 HOUR 10 MINUTES

1kg ricotta cheese
5 eggs, beaten lightly
1 tablespoon finely grated lemon rind
¼ cup (60ml) lemon juice
½ teaspoon vanilla extract
1 cup (220g) caster sugar
¼ cup (40g) sultanas
½ cup (125g) finely chopped mixed
   glacé fruit

PASTRY
90g butter, softened
1 egg
¼ cup (55g) caster sugar
1¼ cups (185g) plain flour
¼ cup (35g) self-raising flour

1 Grease 25cm springform tin.
2 Make pastry.
3 Reduce oven temperature to moderately slow.
4 Blend or process cheese, eggs, rind, juice, extract and sugar until smooth. Stir in sultanas and glacé fruit; pour cheesecake filling over pastry base.
5 Bake cheesecake, uncovered, in moderately slow oven about 50 minutes or until filling sets; cool at room temperature, then refrigerate until cold.

PASTRY Beat butter in small bowl with electric mixer until smooth; add egg and sugar, beating until just combined. Stir in half of the combined sifted flours; work remaining flour in by hand. Knead pastry gently on floured surface until smooth. Cover with plastic wrap; refrigerate 30 minutes. Preheat oven to moderately hot. Roll pastry between sheets of baking paper until large enough to cover base of prepared tin. Lift pastry into tin; press into base. Lightly prick pastry with fork, cover; refrigerate 30 minutes. Bake, uncovered, in moderately hot oven 20 minutes.

serves 16
tip This recipe is best made a day ahead and stored, covered, in the refrigerator overnight.

PAVLOVA

PREPARATION TIME 20 MINUTES **COOKING TIME** 1 HOUR 15 MINUTES

4 egg whites
1 cup (220g) caster sugar
1 tablespoon cornflour
1 teaspoon white vinegar
300ml thickened cream
1 teaspoon vanilla extract
1 tablespoon icing sugar mixture
150g strawberries, sliced thinly
150g blueberries
120g raspberries

1 Preheat oven to very slow. Grease and line oven tray with baking paper;
trace an 18cm circle on paper.
2 Beat egg whites in small bowl with electric mixer until soft peaks form.
Gradually add caster sugar, a tablespoon at a time, beating until sugar
dissolves between additions. Fold in cornflour and vinegar.
3 Spread meringue inside circle on prepared tray; level top with spatula.
Bake, uncovered, in very slow oven about 1¼ hours or until meringue
is firm. Cool meringue in oven with door ajar.
4 Beat cream, extract and icing sugar in small bowl with electric mixer until
soft peaks form. Serve meringue topped with cream mixture and fruit.

serves 8
tips If you prefer not to accompany the pavlova with berries, you can
use kiwi fruit, thinly sliced pineapple, pawpaw and passionfruit pulp.
Pavlova meringue can be made up to 4 days ahead, then filled up to
1 hour before serving.

BLACKBERRY AND ORANGE MASCARPONE CAKE

PREPARATION TIME 30 MINUTES (PLUS REFRIGERATION TIME) **COOKING TIME** 50 MINUTES

185g butter
1 tablespoon finely grated orange rind
1 cup (220g) caster sugar
3 eggs, beaten lightly
1 cup (150g) self-raising flour
1/3 cup (40g) almond meal
1/2 cup (125ml) orange juice
350g blackberries
1/3 cup (110g) blackberry jam, warmed
1 tablespoon orange-flavoured liqueur
1 tablespoon icing sugar mixture

MASCARPONE CREAM

2/3 cup (160ml) thickened cream
1 cup (250g) mascarpone cheese
1/3 cup (55g) icing sugar mixture
1 teaspoon finely grated orange rind
1 tablespoon orange-flavoured liqueur

1 Preheat oven to moderately slow. Grease deep 22cm-round cake pan; line base and side with baking paper.

2 Beat butter, rind and caster sugar in medium bowl with electric mixer until light and fluffy. Add eggs, one at a time, beating until combined between additions. Fold flour, almond meal and juice, in two batches, into butter mixture.

3 Pour cake mixture into prepared pan; bake, uncovered, in moderately slow oven about 50 minutes. Stand cake 5 minutes, then turn onto wire rack; turn cake top-side up to cool.

4 Meanwhile, make mascarpone cream.

5 Reserve 10 blackberries. Using large serrated knife, split cake into three layers. Place one layer of cake on serving plate; spread with half of the combined jam and liqueur. Spread with half of the mascarpone cream, then top with half of the blackberries. Repeat layering process, finishing with layer of cake. Cover; refrigerate 1 hour. Serve cake sprinkled with sifted icing sugar and reserved blackberries.
MASCARPONE CREAM Beat cream, cheese and sugar in small bowl with electric mixer until soft peaks form; stir in rind and liqueur.

serves 10
tip You can use Cointreau, Grand Marnier, Curaçao or any other orange-flavoured liqueur in this recipe.

CHOCOLATE, NUT AND COFFEE ICE-CREAM CAKE

PREPARATION TIME 35 MINUTES (PLUS FREEZING TIME)

Vienna almonds are toffee-coated almonds available from selected supermarkets, nut stands and specialty confectionery stores. Crème de cacao is a chocolate-flavoured liqueur found in most liquor stores.

2 litres vanilla ice-cream
1 tablespoon instant coffee powder
1 tablespoon hot water
½ cup (70g) vienna almonds, chopped coarsely
100g dark eating chocolate, melted
1 tablespoon crème de cacao
100g white eating chocolate, melted
½ cup (75g) roasted shelled pistachios, chopped coarsely

1 Grease 21cm springform tin; line base and side with baking paper.

2 Divide ice-cream into three portions; return two portions to freezer. Soften remaining ice-cream in medium bowl.

3 Dissolve coffee in the water in small jug; stir into softened ice-cream with two-thirds of the almonds. Spoon into prepared tin, cover; freeze about 2 hours or until firm.

4 Meanwhile, soften second portion of the ice-cream in medium bowl; stir in dark chocolate. Microwave, uncovered, on MEDIUM-HIGH (80%) about 2 minutes or until chocolate melts; whisk until smooth. Stir in liqueur, cover; freeze about 1 hour or until almost firm. Spoon dark chocolate ice-cream over coffee layer, cover; freeze about 2 hours or until firm.

5 Soften remaining ice-cream in medium bowl; fold in white chocolate. Microwave, uncovered, on MEDIUM-HIGH (80%) about 2 minutes or until chocolate melts; whisk until smooth. Stir in two-thirds of the pistachios, cover; freeze about 1 hour or until almost firm, stirring ice-cream occasionally to suspend pistachios evenly. Spoon white chocolate ice-cream over dark chocolate layer, cover; freeze about 2 hours or until firm.

6 Remove ice-cream cake from tin just before serving; sprinkle with remaining almonds and pistachios.

serves 10

tips Use a good-quality ice-cream; various ice-creams differ, according to manufacturer, depending on the quantities of air and fat incorporated into the mixture. It's important that each layer sets before adding the next. To help remove ice-cream cake, rub sides of tin with hot cloth.

SPARKLING STONE FRUIT AND RASPBERRY JELLY

PREPARATION TIME 15 MINUTES (PLUS REFRIGERATION TIME) **COOKING TIME** 10 MINUTES

½ cup (110g) caster sugar
1 bottle (750ml) sweet
   sparkling wine
1½ tablespoons gelatine
½ cup (125ml) water
2 tablespoons lemon juice
1 medium nectarine (170g),
   sliced thinly
2 medium apricots (100g),
   sliced thinly
1 medium plum (110g),
   sliced thinly
200g raspberries

1 Stir sugar and 1 cup of the wine
   in medium saucepan over heat,
   without boiling, until sugar
   dissolves; bring to a boil. Reduce
   heat; simmer, uncovered, without
   stirring, 5 minutes.
2 Meanwhile, sprinkle gelatine over
   the water in small heatproof
   jug; stand jug in small saucepan
   of simmering water. Stir until
   gelatine dissolves. Stir gelatine
   mixture, remaining wine and juice
   into wine mixture.
3 Divide fruit among six 1-cup
   (250ml) serving glasses. Pour
   wine mixture over fruit. Cover;
   refrigerate until firm.

serves 6
tips You can use canned stoned
fruit for this recipe if fresh fruit
is out of season.
It's best to make this recipe
a day in advance.

SUMMER FRUIT IN BLACKCURRANT SYRUP

PREPARATION TIME 10 MINUTES **COOKING TIME** 20 MINUTES

1 vanilla bean
½ cup (125ml) water
1½ cups (375ml) blackcurrant syrup
4 medium apricots (200g)
4 medium plums (450g)
2 medium nectarines (350g), halved
2 medium peaches (300g), halved
200g french vanilla Frûche

1 Split vanilla bean in half lengthways; scrape seeds into medium saucepan. Add pod, the water and syrup to pan; bring to a boil. Boil, uncovered, about 5 minutes or until syrup thickens slightly. Add fruit, reduce heat; simmer, uncovered, turning fruit occasionally, about 8 minutes or until fruit is tender.

2 Remove fruit mixture from heat; discard vanilla bean. Serve fruit and syrup topped with Frûche.

serves 4

CHOC-STRAWBERRY MERINGUE GÂTEAU

PREPARATION TIME 40 MINUTES **COOKING TIME** 45 MINUTES

125g butter
4 eggs, separated
¾ cup (165g) caster sugar
1 cup (150g) self-raising flour
⅓ cup (35g) cocoa powder
½ teaspoon bicarbonate of soda
1 cup (250ml) buttermilk
⅔ cup (150g) caster sugar, extra
¼ cup (30g) coarsely chopped roasted hazelnuts
⅔ cup (160ml) thickened cream
1 tablespoon icing sugar mixture
250g strawberries, halved

1 Preheat oven to moderately slow. Grease two 20cm sandwich pans; line bases and sides with baking paper.

2 Beat butter, egg yolks and caster sugar in medium bowl with electric mixer until light and fluffy. Stir in combined sifted flour, cocoa and soda, then buttermilk. Divide mixture between prepared pans.

3 Beat egg whites in small bowl with electric mixer until soft peaks form; gradually add extra caster sugar, a tablespoon at a time, beating until sugar dissolves between additions.

4 Divide meringue mixture over cake mixture in pans; using spatula, spread meringue so cake mixture is completely covered. Sprinkle nuts over meringue mixture on one of the cakes. Bake cakes, uncovered, in moderately slow oven 25 minutes. Cover pans loosely with foil; bake in moderately slow oven about 20 minutes. Stand cakes in pans 5 minutes, turn onto wire racks; turn cakes top-side up to cool.

5 Beat cream and icing sugar mixture in small bowl with electric mixer until soft peaks form. Place cake without nuts on serving plate; spread with cream mixture. Sprinkle with strawberries; top with remaining cake.

serves 12
tip This recipe is best made on the day of serving.

CHOCOLATE NOUGAT FROZEN PARFAIT

PREPARATION TIME 20 MINUTES (PLUS FREEZING TIME)

2¼ cups (450g) ricotta cheese
½ cup (110g) caster sugar
200g dark eating
  chocolate, melted
150g almond nougat,
  chopped coarsely
300ml thickened cream

1 Grease 14cm x 21cm loaf pan;
  line base and two long sides with
  baking paper, extending paper
  5cm above edges of pan.
2 Blend or process cheese and
  sugar until smooth; transfer to
  medium bowl. Stir in chocolate
  and nougat.
3 Beat cream in small bowl
  with electric mixer until soft
  peaks form. Fold cream into
  chocolate mixture.
4 Spoon mixture into prepared pan,
  cover with foil; freeze overnight.
5 Remove parfait from pan; slice
  thickly. Stand 10 minutes
  before serving.

serves 8
serving suggestion Serve with
fresh raspberries, if desired.

EASY PASSIONFRUIT COCONUT TART

PREPARATION TIME 15 MINUTES **COOKING TIME** 45 MINUTES
You need about six passionfruit for this recipe.

1 cup (90g) desiccated coconut
¾ cup (165g) caster sugar
½ cup (75g) plain flour
4 eggs, beaten lightly
1⅓ cups (330ml) milk
125g butter, melted
½ cup (125ml)
 passionfruit pulp
1 tablespoon lemon juice
2 tablespoons icing
 sugar mixture

1 Preheat oven to moderate. Grease
 24cm pie dish.
2 Combine coconut, sugar and flour
 in large jug; stir in combined
 egg, milk, butter, passionfruit
 and juice.
3 Pour mixture into prepared dish.
 Bake, uncovered, in moderate
 oven about 45 minutes or until
 set; cool in dish. Serve tart
 dusted with sifted icing sugar.

serves 8
tip You can also use canned
passionfruit pulp for this recipe.

DECADENT CHOCOLATE ROULADE

PREPARATION TIME 15 MINUTES (PLUS REFRIGERATION TIME)
COOKING TIME 15 MINUTES

200g dark eating chocolate, chopped coarsely
¼ cup (60ml) hot water
1 teaspoon instant coffee powder
4 eggs, separated
¾ cup (165g) caster sugar
300ml thickened cream
150g raspberries

1 Preheat oven to moderate. Grease 25cm x 30cm swiss roll pan; line base and long sides with baking paper, extending paper 5cm above edges of pan.
2 Combine chocolate, the water and coffee powder in large heatproof bowl. Stir over large saucepan of simmering water until smooth; remove from heat.
3 Beat egg yolks and ½ cup of the sugar in small bowl with electric mixer about 5 minutes or until thick and creamy; fold egg mixture into warm chocolate mixture.
4 Beat egg whites in small bowl with electric mixer until soft peaks form; fold egg whites, in two batches, into chocolate mixture. Spread into prepared pan; bake, uncovered, in moderate oven about 10 minutes.
5 Meanwhile, place a piece of baking paper cut the same size as swiss roll pan on board; sprinkle evenly with remaining sugar. Turn cake onto sugared paper; peel lining paper away. Cool.
6 Beat cream in small bowl of electric mixer until firm peaks form. Spread cream over cake; sprinkle with raspberries. Roll cake, from long side, by lifting paper and using it to guide the roll into shape. Cover roll; refrigerate 30 minutes before serving.

serves 8
tips Chocolate mixture is suitable to microwave.
Be sure you beat the egg whites only until soft peaks form. Overbeating will dry out the egg whites and make them difficult to fold into chocolate mixture.
The roulade can be made 1 day in advance, then filled and rolled 6 hours in advance.

RASPBERRY SORBET

PREPARATION TIME 15 MINUTES (PLUS FREEZING TIME) **COOKING TIME** 10 MINUTES

1 cup (250ml) water
1 cup (220g) caster sugar
600g frozen raspberries
1 tablespoon lemon juice
2 egg whites

1 Stir the water and sugar in small saucepan over heat, without boiling, until sugar dissolves; bring to a boil. Reduce heat, simmer, uncovered, without stirring, 5 minutes.

2 Blend or process raspberries, juice and hot sugar mixture until smooth.

3 Push mixture through fine sieve into 20cm x 30cm lamington pan; discard seeds. Cover with foil; freeze until firm.

4 Chop frozen berry mixture coarsely. Blend or process with egg whites until smooth and paler in colour. Return mixture to pan, cover; freeze until firm.

serves 6

tips This recipe can be made a week in advance.
Raspberries may be replaced with any other berry.
If using an ice-cream churner, combine fruit puree with egg whites; churn following manufacturer's instructions.

MANGO AND PASSIONFRUIT FOOL

PREPARATION TIME 15 MINUTES (PLUS REFRIGERATION TIME)
You need one passionfruit for this recipe.

1 large mango (600g),
chopped coarsely
1 tablespoon passionfruit pulp
2 egg whites
¹⁄₃ cup (75g) caster sugar
400g vanilla yogurt

1 Blend or process mango until smooth. Combine mango puree and passionfruit in small bowl.
2 Beat egg whites in small bowl with electric mixer until soft peaks form. Gradually add sugar, 1 tablespoon at a time, beating until sugar dissolves between additions. Gently fold yogurt into egg-white mixture.
3 Layer mango mixture and egg-white mixture into four 1½-cup (375ml) serving glasses. Cover; refrigerate 30 minutes before serving.

serves 4
tip Frozen mango puree can be used if mangoes are out of season.

CHOCOLATE GANACHE AND RASPBERRY CAKE

PREPARATION TIME 25 MINUTES **COOKING TIME** 1 HOUR 25 MINUTES

⅓ cup (35g) cocoa powder
⅓ cup (80ml) water
150g dark eating chocolate, melted
150g butter, melted
1⅓ cups (300g) firmly packed brown sugar
1 cup (125g) almond meal
4 eggs, separated
200g dark eating chocolate, chopped coarsely
⅔ cup (160ml) thickened cream
300g raspberries

1 Preheat oven to moderately slow. Grease deep 22cm-round cake pan; line base and side with baking paper.
2 Blend sifted cocoa with the water in large bowl until smooth. Stir in melted chocolate, butter, sugar, almond meal and egg yolks.
3 Beat egg whites in small bowl with electric mixer until soft peaks form. Fold egg whites, in two batches, into chocolate mixture.
4 Pour mixture into prepared pan; bake, uncovered, in moderately slow oven about 1¼ hours. Stand cake 15 minutes, then turn onto wire rack; turn cake top-side up to cool.
5 Stir chopped chocolate and cream in small saucepan over low heat until smooth.
6 Place raspberries on top of cake; drizzle chocolate mixture over raspberries. Stand cake at room temperature until chocolate sets.

serves 12
tips Undecorated cake is suitable to freeze.
The cake can be made up to 3 days in advance. Top cake with raspberries and chocolate on the day of serving. Chocolate and butter can be combined and melted in a saucepan over low heat or in a microwave oven. Chopped chocolate and cream can be heated together in a microwave oven.

APRICOT AND WHITE CHOCOLATE TRUFFLES

PREPARATION TIME 30 MINUTES (PLUS STANDING AND REFRIGERATION TIMES)
You will need two lemons for this recipe.

2¾ cups (410g) dried apricots
1 cup (250ml) boiling water
60g butter, softened
½ cup (80g) icing
   sugar mixture
1½ cups (135g)
   desiccated coconut
1 tablespoon finely grated
   lemon rind
180g white eating
   chocolate, melted
4 cups (600g) white chocolate
   Melts, melted

1 Grease 20cm x 30cm lamington
   pan; line base and long sides with
   baking paper.
2 Combine apricots and the water
   in medium heatproof bowl. Cover;
   stand 30 minutes, drain.
3 Blend or process apricots, butter,
   sugar, coconut, rind and white
   chocolate until combined. Spread
   mixture in prepared pan, cover;
   refrigerate overnight.
4 Roll rounded teaspoons of the
   mixture into balls, place on
   baking-paper-lined tray. Dip
   balls in a third of the Melts;
   roll quickly and gently between
   palms to coat evenly. Return balls
   to tray; refrigerate until firm.
   Repeat process twice more with
   remaining Melts to give balls two
   more white coats.

makes 65
tips Recipe can be made up
to 1 week in advance.
White chocolate and white
chocolate Melts are suitable
to microwave.

HOT RASPBERRY SOUFFLÉS

PREPARATION TIME 15 MINUTES **COOKING TIME** 25 MINUTES

300g frozen raspberries, thawed
1 tablespoon water
½ cup (110g) caster sugar
4 egg whites
300ml thickened cream
2 teaspoons caster sugar, extra

1 Preheat oven to moderate. Grease four 1-cup (250ml) ovenproof dishes; place on oven tray.

2 Combine 250g of the raspberries and the water in small saucepan; bring to a boil. Reduce heat; simmer, uncovered, until raspberries soften. Add sugar, stir over medium heat, without boiling, until sugar dissolves; bring to a boil. Reduce heat; simmer, uncovered, about 5 minutes or until mixture is thick and pulpy. Remove from heat; push mixture through fine sieve over small bowl, discard seeds.

3 Beat egg whites in small bowl with electric mixer until soft peaks form. With motor operating, gradually add hot raspberry mixture; beat until well combined.

4 Divide mixture among prepared dishes. Bake, uncovered, in moderate oven about 15 minutes or until soufflés are puffed and browned lightly.

5 Meanwhile, beat remaining raspberries, cream and extra sugar in small bowl with electric mixer until thickened slightly. Serve hot soufflés with raspberry cream.

serves 4
tip Thaw raspberries on absorbent paper in the refrigerator.

WHITE CHOCOLATE MUD CAKE

PREPARATION TIME 50 MINUTES (PLUS COOLING TIME) **COOKING TIME** 1 HOUR 45 MINUTES

250g butter, chopped
180g white eating chocolate,
  chopped coarsely
1½ cups (330g) caster sugar
¾ cup (180ml) milk
1½ cups (225g) plain flour
½ cup (75g) self-raising flour
½ teaspoon vanilla extract
2 eggs, beaten lightly

WHITE CHOCOLATE GANACHE
½ cup (125ml) thickened cream
360g white eating chocolate,
  chopped finely

CHOCOLATE CURLS
1⅓ cups (200g) dark chocolate
  Melts, melted
1⅓ cups (200g) white
  chocolate Melts, melted
1⅓ cups (200g) milk chocolate
  Melts, melted

1 Preheat oven to moderately slow. Grease deep 20cm-round cake pan; line base and side with baking paper.
2 Combine butter, chocolate, sugar and milk in medium saucepan; stir over low heat until melted. Transfer mixture to large bowl; cool 15 minutes.
3 Stir in sifted flours, extract and egg; pour into prepared pan. Bake, uncovered, in moderately slow oven about 1 hour 40 minutes; cool cake in pan.
4 Meanwhile, make white chocolate ganache and chocolate curls.
5 Turn cake onto serving plate top-side up. Spread ganache all over cake; top with chocolate curls.
  WHITE CHOCOLATE GANACHE Bring cream to a boil in small saucepan; pour over chocolate in medium bowl, stir with wooden spoon until chocolate melts. Cover bowl; refrigerate, stirring occasionally, about 30 minutes or until ganache is of a spreadable consistency.
  CHOCOLATE CURLS Spread dark, white and milk chocolate separately on marble slab or bench top. When chocolate is almost set, drag ice-cream scoop over surface of chocolate to make curls. Set chocolate can be scraped up, re-melted and used again.

serves 12

Spread melted chocolate on cool surface such as a marble board.

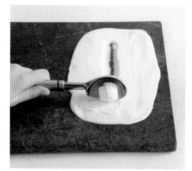

When almost set, drag ice-cream scoop over chocolate to make curls.

Decorate cake with alternate dark, white and milk chocolate curls.

RHUBARB CRUMBLE ICE-CREAM

PREPARATION TIME 10 MINUTES (PLUS FREEZING TIME)
COOKING TIME 10 MINUTES
This recipe can be made 1 week in advance.

2 cups (220g) chopped rhubarb
2 tablespoons brown sugar
2 litres vanilla ice-cream, softened slightly
125g Ginger Nut biscuits, chopped coarsely

1 Line 14cm x 21cm loaf pan with plastic wrap.
2 Cook rhubarb and sugar in large heavy-based saucepan, covered, about 5 minutes or until rhubarb is almost tender. Reduce heat; simmer, uncovered, about 5 minutes or until rhubarb softens but retains shape. Cool.
3 Place ice-cream in large bowl; break up slightly. Gently swirl in biscuits and rhubarb mixture.
4 Pour ice-cream mixture into prepared pan. Cover; freeze 3 hours or until firm.

serves 8

FRESH PINEAPPLE WITH COCONUT

PREPARATION TIME 10 MINUTES
You need about four passionfruit for this recipe.

1 small pineapple (800g)
⅓ cup (80ml) passionfruit pulp
2 tablespoons coconut-flavoured liqueur
¼ cup (10g) flaked coconut, toasted

1 Peel and core pineapple; slice thinly.
2 Divide pineapple among serving dishes; drizzle with passionfruit and liqueur, sprinkle with coconut.

serves 4
tip We used Malibu in this recipe, but you can use any rum-based coconut-flavoured liqueur.

ICE-CREAM WITH ESPRESSO AND IRISH CREAM

PREPARATION TIME 15 MINUTES

2 tablespoons finely ground espresso coffee
²/₃ cup (160ml) boiling water
500ml vanilla ice-cream
½ cup (125ml) irish cream liqueur
4 chocolate-coated rolled wafer sticks (15g)

1 Place coffee and the water in coffee plunger; stand 2 minutes, plunge coffee. Cool 5 minutes.
2 Divide ice-cream among serving glasses; pour liqueur then coffee over ice-cream. Serve with wafer sticks.

serves 4
tip We used Bailey's Irish Cream in this recipe, but you can use any irish cream liqueur.

GRILLED BANANAS WITH VANILLA CREAM

PREPARATION TIME 10 MINUTES
COOKING TIME 10 MINUTES

4 medium bananas (800g), halved lengthways
¼ cup (55g) brown sugar
20g butter
2 tablespoons coconut-flavoured liqueur
1 vanilla bean
²/₃ cup (160ml) thickened cream
1 tablespoon icing sugar mixture

1 Sprinkle banana with 1 tablespoon of the brown sugar; place under hot grill until browned lightly.
2 Meanwhile, stir remaining brown sugar, butter and liqueur in small saucepan over low heat until smooth.
3 Split vanilla bean in half lengthways, scrape seeds into small bowl; discard pod. Add cream and icing sugar; beat with electric mixer until soft peaks form.
4 Serve banana with vanilla cream; drizzle with sauce.

serves 4

glossary

ALMOND flat, ovoid nut with pitted brown shell enclosing a creamy white kernel encased in a paper-thin brown skin.

essence a synthetically produced substance used sparingly to impart an almond flavour to foods.

flaked paper-thin slices.

meal also known as ground almonds; the nut is powdered to a flour-like texture, for use in baking or as a thickening agent.

nougat made from sugar, glucose, almonds, egg white and gelatine.

vienna toffee-coated nut.

BAKING POWDER raising agent consisting mainly of two parts cream of tartar to one part bicarbonate of soda.

BICARBONATE OF SODA also known as baking soda.

BLACKCURRANT SYRUP we used Ribena, but you can use any blackcurrant syrup.

BRANDY spirit distilled from wine.

BUTTER use salted or unsalted ("sweet") butter; 125g is equal to 1 stick of butter.

BUTTERMILK sold with other fresh milk products in the refrigerated sections in supermarkets; made commercially by a method similar to yogurt. Despite the implication of its name, it is low in fat and is a good substitute for dairy products such as cream or sour cream; it is particularly good in baking and in salad dressings.

CARDAMOM native to India and used extensively in its cuisine; can be purchased in pod, seed or ground form. Has a distinctively aromatic, sweetly rich flavour, and is one of the world's most expensive spices.

CHOCOLATE

dark eating made of cocoa liquor, cocoa butter and sugar.

Melts discs made of milk, white or dark chocolate compound; good for melting and moulding.

milk eating the high milk solids content does not recommend it for baking.

CINNAMON STICK dried inner bark of the shoots of a cinnamon tree.

CLOVES dried flower buds of a tropical tree; can be used whole or in ground form. Have a strong scent and taste so should be used minimally.

COCOA POWDER also known simply as cocoa; dried, roasted then ground, unsweetened cocoa beans.

COCONUT

desiccated unsweetened, concentrated, dried then shredded coconut.

flaked dried flaked coconut flesh.

shredded thin strips of dried coconut flesh.

COFFEE-FLAVOURED LIQUEUR Tia Maria, Kahlúa or any generic brand.

COINTREAU a sweet and bitter citrus-flavoured, clear French liqueur.

CORNFLOUR also known as cornstarch; used as a thickening agent in cooking.

CRAISINS dried cranberries.

CREAM

sour (minimum fat content 35%) a thick commercially cultured soured cream.

thickened (minimum fat content 35%) a whipping cream containing gelatine as a thickener.

CREAM CHEESE commonly known as Philadelphia or Philly, a soft cow-milk cheese with a fat content of at least 33%. Sold both in bulk and in packages.

CREAM OF TARTAR the acid ingredient in baking powder; added to confectionery mixtures to help prevent sugar crystallising. Keeps frostings creamy and improves volume when beating egg whites.

CUSTARD POWDER instant mixture used to make pouring custard; similar to North American instant pudding mixes.

DARK RUM we prefer to use an underproof rum (not overproof) for a more subtle flavour.

EGG some recipes call for raw or barely cooked eggs; exercise caution if salmonella is a problem in your area.

FIGS (DRIED) the slightly crunchy, dehydrated form of a black or golden fruit. They can be eaten as is or used as an ingredient in savoury dishes or desserts.

FLOUR

plain an all-purpose flour, made from wheat.

self-raising plain flour sifted with baking powder in the proportion of 1 cup of flour to 2 teaspoons of baking powder.

GELATINE (GELATIN) we used powdered gelatine as a setting agent. It is also available in sheets called leaf gelatine.

GLACÉ FRUIT mixed fruits cooked in a heavy sugar syrup then dried.

GLACÉ PINEAPPLE pineapple that has been cooked in a heavy sugar syrup then dried.

GRAND MARNIER an orange-flavoured liqueur that is brandy-based.

HAZELNUT also known as a filbert; plump, grape-sized, rich, sweet nut with a brown inedible skin that is removed by rubbing heated nuts together vigorously in a tea towel.

ICE-CREAM we used a middle-range ice-cream with 5g of fat per 100ml; ice-creams differ between manufacturers, depending on the quantities of air and fat incorporated into the mixture.

JAM also known as preserve or conserve.

KAHLÚA a coffee-flavoured liqueur from Mexico.

LAMINGTON PAN slab cake pan measuring 20cm x 30cm, 3cm deep.

macadamias

MACADAMIAS native to Australia; this rich, buttery nut should be stored in the refrigerator because of its high oil content.

MAPLE SYRUP a thin syrup distilled from the sap of the maple tree.

MARSALA a sweet fortified wine originally from Sicily.

MASCARPONE CHEESE a fresh, unripened, thick,

ground cardamom

cardamom seeds

cardamom pods

black cardamom pods

triple-cream cheese with a delicately sweet, slightly acidic flavour.

MILK we used full-cream homogenised milk unless otherwise specified.

sweetened condensed a canned milk product consisting of milk with more than half the water content removed and sugar added to the milk that remains.

MIXED SPICE a blend of ground spices usually consisting of cinnamon, allspice and nutmeg.

PEACH SCHNAPPS a strong, dry, colourless alcoholic spirit made from potatoes or grains and the distillation of peaches.

PECANS native to the United States and now grown locally; dark golden-brown in colour, buttery and rich in flavour. Good in savoury or sweet dishes; especially good in salads.

PISTACHIO pale green, delicately flavoured nut inside a hard off-white shell. To peel, soak shelled nuts in boiling water for about 5 minutes; drain then pat dry with absorbent paper. Rub the skins with cloth to peel.

RICOTTA CHEESE soft white cow-milk cheese; roughly translates as "cooked again". It's made from whey, a by-product of other cheese-making, to which fresh milk and acid are added. Ricotta is a sweet, moist cheese with a fat content of around 8.5% and a slightly grainy texture.

RIND also known as zest; the edible thin outer layer of citrus fruits.

ROSEWATER extract made from crushed rose petals, called gulab in India; used for its aromatic quality in many desserts.

sago

SAGO also known as seed or pearl tapioca, it is from the sago palm, while tapioca is from the root of the cassava plant. Used in soups and desserts, often as a thickening agent.

vanilla bean

vanilla bean seeds

as an ingredient in cooking and as a condiment. To toast, spread seeds evenly on oven tray; toast briefly in moderate oven.

SHERRY fortified wine consumed as an aperitif or used in cooking. Sold as fino (dry, light), amontillado (medium-sweet, dark) and oloroso (full-bodied, very dark).

STALE BREADCRUMBS bread that is one or two days old made into crumbs by grating, blending or processing.

SUGAR we used coarse, granulated table sugar, also known as crystal sugar, unless otherwise specified.

SULTANAS also known as golden raisins; dried seedless white grapes.

TIA MARIA a coffee-flavoured liqueur from Jamaica.

TOBLERONE brand name of famous Swiss chocolate containing honey and almond nougat.

VANILLA

bean dried, long, thin pod from a tropical golden orchid grown in Central and South America and Tahiti; the tiny black seeds inside the bean are used to impart a luscious vanilla flavour in baking and desserts.

essence obtained from vanilla beans infused in alcohol and water.

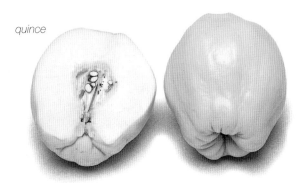
quince

savoiardi

PLAIN SWEET BISCUITS un-iced biscuits or cookies used to make crumbs.

QUINCE yellow-skinned fruit with hard texture and tart, astringent taste; always cooked, often as a preserve.

RAISIN dried sweet grape.

READY-ROLLED PUFF PASTRY packaged sheets of frozen puff pastry, available from most supermarkets.

SAVOIARDI also known as savoy biscuits, ladyfingers or sponge finger biscuits, these are Italian-style crisp fingers made from sponge cake mixture.

SESAME SEEDS black and white are the most common forms of this small oval seed, however there are red and brown varieties also. A good source of calcium; used in cuisines the world over

brown a soft, finely granulated sugar containing molasses to give it its characteristic colour.

caster also known as superfine or finely granulated table sugar.

demerara small-grained, golden crystal sugar.

icing sugar mixture also known as confectioners' or powdered sugar; crushed granulated sugar with about 3% added cornflour.

pure icing also known as confectioners' sugar but without the cornflour.

extract obtained from vanilla beans infused in water. A non-alcoholic version of essence.

extract, concentrated essence that has been reduced in a sugar syrup to a more concentrated form. Use 1:2 in place of essence/extract or 2:1 in place of beans.

WALNUT crisp-textured nut with a crinkled surface and an astringent flavour.

WHEATEN CORNFLOUR made with wheat instead of corn; available from most supermarkets.

index

facts & figures

Wherever you live, you'll be able to use our recipes with the help of these easy-to-follow conversions. While these conversions are approximate only, the difference between an exact and the approximate conversion of various liquid and dry measures is minimal and will not affect cooking results.

liquid measures

metric	imperial
30ml	1 fluid oz
60ml	2 fluid oz
100ml	3 fluid oz
125ml	4 fluid oz
150ml	5 fluid oz (¼ pint/1 gill)
190ml	6 fluid oz
250ml	8 fluid oz
300ml	10 fluid oz (½ pint)
500ml	16 fluid oz
600ml	20 fluid oz (1 pint)
1000ml (1 litre)	1¾ pints

dry measures

metric	imperial
15g	½oz
30g	1oz
60g	2oz
90g	3oz
125g	4oz (¼lb)
155g	5oz
185g	6oz
220g	7oz
250g	8oz (½lb)
280g	9oz
315g	10oz
345g	11oz
375g	12oz (¾lb)
410g	13oz
440g	14oz
470g	15oz
500g	16oz (1lb)
750g	24oz (1½lb)
1kg	32oz (2lb)

helpful measures

metric	imperial
3mm	⅛in
6mm	¼in
1cm	½in
2cm	¾in
2.5cm	1in
5cm	2in
6cm	2½in
8cm	3in
10cm	4in
13cm	5in
15cm	6in
18cm	7in
20cm	8in
23cm	9in
25cm	10in
28cm	11in
30cm	12in (1ft)

measuring equipment

The difference between one country's measuring cups and another's is, at most, within a 2 or 3 teaspoon variance. (For the record, 1 Australian metric measuring cup holds approximately 250ml.) The most accurate way of measuring dry ingredients is to weigh them. When measuring liquids, use a clear glass or plastic jug with metric markings. (For the record, 1 Australian metric tablespoon holds 20ml; 1 Australian metric teaspoon holds 5ml.)

Note: NZ, Canada, US and UK use 15ml tablespoons. All cup and spoon measurements are level.

We use large eggs with an average weight of 60g.

how to measure

When using graduated metric measuring cups, shake dry ingredients loosely into the appropriate cup. Do not tap the cup on a bench or tightly pack the ingredients unless directed to do so. Level top of measuring cups and measuring spoons with a knife. When measuring liquids, place a clear glass or plastic jug with metric markings on a flat surface to check accuracy at eye level.

oven temperatures

These oven temperatures are only a guide. Always check the manufacturer's manual.

	°C (Celsius)	°F (Fahrenheit)	Gas Mark
Very slow	120	250	1
Slow	150	300	2
Moderately slow	160	325	3
Moderate	180 – 190	350 – 375	4
Moderately hot	200 – 210	400 – 425	5
Hot	220 – 230	450 – 475	6
Very hot	240 – 250	500 – 525	7

Looking after **your interest...**

Keep your ACP cookbooks clean, tidy and within easy reach with slipcovers designed to hold up to 12 books. Plus you can follow our recipes perfectly with a set of accurate measuring cups and spoons, as used by *The Australian Women's Weekly* Test Kitchen.

To order

Mail or fax Photocopy and complete the coupon below and post to ACP Books Reader Offer, ACP Publishing, GPO Box 4967, Sydney NSW 2001, or fax to (02) 9267 4967.

Phone Have your credit card details ready, then phone 136 116 (Mon-Fri, 8.00am-6.00pm; Sat, 8.00am-6.00pm).

Price

Book Holder

Australia: $13.10 (incl. GST).
Elsewhere: $A21.95.

Metric Measuring Set

Australia: $6.50 (incl. GST).
New Zealand: $A8.00.
Elsewhere: $A9.95.

Prices include postage and handling.
This offer is available in all countries.

Payment

Australian residents

We accept the credit cards listed on the coupon, money orders and cheques.

Overseas residents

We accept the credit cards listed on the coupon, drafts in $A drawn on an Australian bank, and also UK, NZ and US cheques in the currency of the country of issue. Credit card charges are at the exchange rate current at the time of payment.

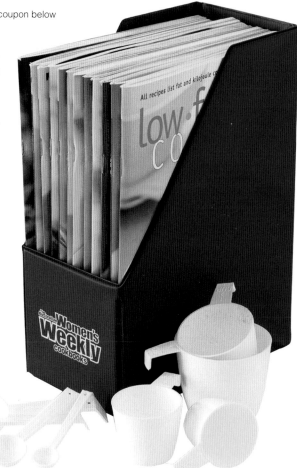

Test Kitchen
Food director *Pamela Clark*
Food editor *Karen Hammial*
Assistant food editor *Amira Ibram*
Test Kitchen manager *Kimberley Coverdale*
Senior home economist *Cathie Lonnie*
Home economists *Sammie Coryton,
Nancy Duran, Elizabeth Macri,
Christina Martignago, Susie Riggall,
Kirrily Smith, Kate Tait, Vanessa Vetter*
Editorial coordinator *Rebecca Steyns*
The Australian Women's Weekly
Food director *Lyndey Milan*
Food editor *Alexandra McCowan*
Deputy food editor *Frances Abdallaoui*
Photographers: *Alan Benson, Joe Filshie, Chr
Jones, Andre Martin, Brett Stevens*
Stylists: *Marie-Helene Clauzon,
Georgina Dolling, Carolyn Fienberg,
Jane Hann, Mary Harris, Katy Holder*
Additional photography
Photographer: *Brett Stevens*
Stylists: *Julz Beresford, Opel Khan (p106)*
Home economists: *Elizabeth Macri,
Cathie Lonnie, Nancy Duran, Kirrily Smith*
Photographer (step shots): *Rob Shaw*
Home economist (step shots): *Susie Riggall*
ACP Books
Editorial director *Susan Tomnay*
Creative director *Hieu Chi Nguyen*
Senior editor *Lynda Wilton*
Designer *Caryl Wiggins*
Studio manager *Caryl Wiggins*
Editorial/sales coordinator *Caroline Lowry*
Editorial assistant *Karen Lai*
Publishing manager (sales) *Brian Cearnes*
Publishing manager (rights & new projects)
Jane Hazell
Brand manager *Donna Gianniotis*
Pre-press *Harry Palmer*
Production manager *Carol Currie*
Business manager *Seymour Cohen*
Assistant business analyst *Martin Howes*
Chief executive officer *John Alexander*
Group publisher *Pat Ingram*
Publisher *Sue Wannan*

Produced by ACP Books, Sydney.
Printed by Dai Nippon Printing in Korea.
Published by ACP Publishing Pty Limited,
54 Park St, Sydney; GPO Box 4088,
Sydney, NSW 2001.
Ph: (02) 9282 8618 Fax: (02) 9267 9438.
acpbooks@acp.com.au
www.acpbooks.com.au
To order books, phone 136 116.
Send recipe enquiries to:
recipeenquiries@acp.com.au
AUSTRALIA: Distributed by Network Services
GPO Box 4088, Sydney, NSW 2001.
Ph: (02) 9282 8777 Fax: (02) 9264 3278.
UNITED KINGDOM: Distributed by Australian
Consolidated Press (UK), Moulton Park
Business Centre, Red House Rd,
Moulton Park, Northampton, NN3 6AQ.
Ph: (01604) 497531 Fax: (01604) 497533
acpukltd@aol.com
CANADA: Distributed by Whitecap Books Ltd
351 Lynn Ave, North Vancouver, BC, V7J 2C4.
Ph: (604) 980 9852 Fax: (604) 980 8197
customerservice@whitecap.ca
www.whitecap.ca
NEW ZEALAND: Distributed by Netlink
Distribution Company, ACP Media Centre,
Cnr Fanshawe and Beaumont Streets,
Westhaven, Auckland.
PO Box 47906, Ponsonby, Auckland, NZ.
Ph: (09) 366 9966 ask@ndcnz.co.nz
Clark, Pamela.
The Australian Women's Weekly
Best Food Desserts.
Includes index.
ISBN 1 86396 340 5
1. Desserts. I. Title. II. Title: Best food desserts
III. Title: Australian Women's Weekly.
641.86
© ACP Publishing Pty Limited 2004
ABN 18 053 273 546

Photocopy and complete coupon below

- ☐ **Book Holder**

- ☐ **Metric Measuring Set**
    Please indicate number(s) required.

Mr/Mrs/Ms _____

Address _____

_____

Postcode _____ Country _____

Ph: Business hours (   ) _____

I enclose my cheque/money order for $ _____ payable to ACP Publishing.

OR: please charge my

- ☐ Bankcard   ☐ Visa   ☐ Mastercard
- ☐ Diners Club   ☐ American Express

Card number

Expiry date ____ /____

Cardholder's signature _____

Please allow up to 30 days delivery within Australia.
Allow up to 6 weeks for overseas deliveries.
Both offers expire 31/12/04. HLBFD04